Financial Parenthood
Keys to Raising a Rich Kid

Sheena Robinson

10 9 8 7 6 5 4 3 2   0 1 2 5 1 4

Printed in the United States of America

Cover Art: Charly McCracken
Cover/Author Photo: Candace Hight
Graphic Design: TLS Design
Publishing support provided by: Booklogix Publishing Services, Inc., Alpharetta, GA

This paper meets the requirements of ANSI/NISO Z39.48-1992 (Permanence of Paper)

ISBN 978-0-692-53921-7

I would like to dedicate this book to my daughter, Madison. As I watch her grow, she continues to inspire me to be great.

Knowledge is power. Information is liberating. Education is the premise of progress, in every society, in every family.

– Kofi Annan

Contents

Preface

When you picked up this book, you may have wondered what this book was about. You may have even wondered, "Is it really possible to birth a rich kid in the society we live in today?"

Great question!

Before I entered the financial field seven years ago, I felt like I had no control over my life and I had to accept things for the way that they were. I thought it was normal to live in debt. It wasn't until I entered the financial industry that I realized I didn't have to be born into a rich family in order to be wealthy. I spent my first few years learning financial principles that, if applied, could help make a major difference in the lives of many people.

For the first few years of my career, I spent time teaching other adults the financial information I had learned, and I kept hearing the same phrase, "I wish someone would have shared that information with me when I was younger." I knew there was a need for financial education, but it wasn't until I had my daughter two years ago that I realized the need for a bigger platform to help more parents raise up wealthy kids. I knew I wanted to give my child a better childhood than I had, and I knew other parents who desired to do the same. That's when I decided to write this book to help parents with their transition into financial parenting.

There are many books that help adults try to recover their financial situation, but there are very few books that actually give you a step-by-step guide on how to set your child up for wealth starting from birth. I wanted to be able to reach out to a group of people who are very underserved. With only seventeen states requiring students to take some type of financial course upon graduating high school, there is a great need for financial education in the household.[1]

It is my belief that any child who wants to become wealthy when they are older should have that chance regardless of their social class. Knowledge is power. It is a phrase we often hear but don't really act on. This book was designed to give you the information needed to help your child learn financial knowledge that can help them live a prosperous future.

This book is based on countless interviews with parents, research, and my own personal experience. Much time and effort went into making this book a reality. Reading this book will not only help parents raise financially successful children, but it will also help them transform their own financial situation by becoming a role model for their children.

---

[1] http://www.councilforeconed.org/policy-and-advocacy/survey-of-the-states/

Acknowledgments

I am very humbled to have people in my circle who believe in my talents. Thank you to all my friends and family for their love and support. Thank you to my editors, Kelly Nightingale and Daren Fowler, for helping me reshape my thoughts and making them valuable to the people who read them. Thank you to Ms. Charly McCracken for the amazing book cover. A special thanks to you for purchasing this book to help make a difference in the life of your child. Thank you to Tasha Smith with TLS Design for her dedication to help make this book a reality.

Introduction

As you grow, parents and other adults guide you through life until you are old enough to experience it for yourself. They spend a great amount of time providing for you. Their biggest job is to make sure you have the necessities for survival. The things you learn during your childhood help you to become a well-rounded adult.

When I was younger, I never realized that the things my mom taught me would play such a great role in my life. Things as simple as cleaning my room and washing dishes helped shaped me into a responsible adult. I remember how I thought chores were just her way of punishing me and how I would get upset when I had to do them. Looking back, I realize she was only preparing me to live on my own.

By the time you are ready to leave home, the knowledge you learn as a child should empower you to go out and make a life for yourself. Some people leave home to attend college, join the service, or enter the workforce. Some people are lucky enough to run their own businesses, but the majority of people find themselves in dead-end jobs, just working to survive even if they have a college degree. According to Gallup's 2013 State of the American Workplace Survey, 70 percent of those surveyed either hated their jobs or they were completely disengaged.[2]

This doesn't surprise me considering that many people don't believe they get paid what they are worth. They don't realize that most jobs were not designed to make you rich. In order to

---

[2] http://www.ryot.org/gallup-poll-70-americans-disengaged-jobs/376177

accumulate the wealth many of them desire, they will have to invest their money into financial products that give them positive interest, do something extra on the side, or both. However, instead of saving their money, most people get caught up purchasing things they have always wanted. They don't realize that if they are not careful with their spending habits, they will find themselves in debt.

The cause of debt for many people is applying for credit cards. They begin to overspend because they never sit down to create a budget. As debt begins to pile up, the pressure from bill collectors and bad credit begins to weigh them down. When people start accumulating debt and they don't have enough money to maintain their lifestyle, or they make just enough money to pay their bills, they become frustrated.

Unfortunately, the scenario I just described is the life for many adults. It is not until you get out on your own and start having responsibilities that you realize you never had a conversation growing up about how to actually gain wealth or manage your finances. Because of the lack of education, many people find mismanaging money and living in debt as their way of life.

No one plans to be in debt, but the lack of financial preparation leads you there.

As a child, I was never taught how to make my money work for me. No one took time to teach me how to build wealth, how to avoid the credit card trap, or how to purchase "money-making" assets. It was a subject we just didn't talk about in my household. I got my first credit card at 18 years old and started spending immediately. I formed the "if I want it I can have it" attitude. That attitude sent me right into debt.

#FinancialParenthood

I applied for several credit cards, opened up some lines of credit, and signed up for an installment loan when I bought my car. I was very happy while purchasing different items with the funds. Everything seemed to be fine until it was time to pay the money back. That's when I realized I was spending half my paycheck paying back debt.

As I started talking to others about the issue, they informed me that they had grown up under similar conditions. They were so consumed with trying to maintain certain images that they never thought about the consequences. Most people are "instant people." Instant people only live for the moment and never plan for their future. They are more concerned about their current financial situation, and they don't believe they have enough money to begin saving.

As the lack of financial education continues, the financial illiteracy epidemic continues to spread rapidly throughout the United States. A survey revealed that 96 percent of college-bound students would make different financial decisions if they had financial education.[3] If children were taught how to manage money at an early age and how to make it work for them, so many of the financial issues they face as adults could be prevented.

For most children, the reality is they grow up in households where parents work from paycheck to paycheck. Parents are too busy to take out time to educate their children about money because they are caught up in their own financial struggles. They find themselves one paycheck from being homeless. They have no savings, and

---

[3] http://www.financialeducatorscouncil.org/financial-literacy-statistics/

credit cards become their emergency funds. These habits create a mentality for children that this is how life is supposed to be.

The lack of financial education in the school system has also left children with no direction for their financial future. As a result of schools not filling in for parents, children have a higher chance of making poor financial decisions as they get older. Offering a basic financial or budgeting course could make a major difference in the way students manage their money. Because the government doesn't require schools to teach financial education, many of them don't feel it is their responsibility. Until the schools come on board, parents should take a more active interest in helping their children become financially successful.

Resources exist today that can help set children up for a brighter financial future than most adults had available growing up. With this informational age we live in, it is a good idea for parents to keep up with the latest trends on how the rich are staying wealthy. The best way to become someone you have always wanted to be is to model someone who is already walking in the shoes you want to fill. As a financial educator for the past seven years, I have found that there are so many individuals who miss out on an opportunity to change their family's financial future because they do not have any type of financial education. Most people say they want to become financially independent, but they never take the time to actually find out what it takes to get there. You will find it is hard to get closer to your goals unless you put action behind your thoughts. Many people want to win the lottery, but you cannot win the lottery if you don't purchase a ticket. Results take place once action is put forth.

There should come a time in life when you are tired of just settling and you are determined to make the best life possible for you and your children. Society has a way of labeling us and making us feel that if we don't come from certain families, attend certain colleges, or work certain jobs, we will not become wealthy. Those are all lies. The truth is you could work at McDonald's and I could work for a Fortune 500 Company, and you could still become wealthier than me if you knew the information needed to build wealth and put it into action.

If you are experiencing problems with your finances, you can overcome your situation if you are willing to change. People around you can want it for you, but you make the ultimate decision. You have to practice changing negative habits, and you have to surround yourself with people who want the best for you. You also need to have a burning desire to reach your goals and begin to keep promises to yourself.

Once you make up your mind to follow through on the promises you made, you will begin to take action. Three days after graduating from college, I moved to Atlanta, Georgia. It was such a quick transition for me, but I was hungry for a change. I got my first job working for a Fortune 500 Company two months after moving. I was excited and fortunate to have a salary of $36,000 a year coming out of college. As I started saving my money, I moved out of my aunt's house and got my own house and car.

Months passed as I spent money on things I needed and wanted. Eventually, my attitude about work began to change. After I started accumulating things that I thought I couldn't live without and the bills started rolling in, I felt like the job was not paying me enough. It didn't help that I had negative coworkers who were always

#FinancialParenthood

complaining about how they needed more money. Their attitudes began to rub off on me.

I was very open-minded and always knew I wanted more out of life than what I was doing. I remember the day one of my friends invited me to a workshop to learn how to make my money work for me. My whole mentality began to change. I was so intrigued with everything I was learning. After hearing the information, I began to research and explore different ways to put my money to work for me. That's when I decided I wanted to become an entrepreneur. It was the best decision I have ever made, and the rest is history.

I made a personal decision that day after learning I could have a better life for myself. I began to take an interest in me and what I really wanted in life. I realized that if I had been taught as a child about paying myself and other financial principles that would lead to wealth, I would have been set up for a better financial future sooner. We know a lot of things as adults, but we fail to be where we want to be because we fail to put things into action. What good is it to learn something that could make your life better and not apply it? Think about your life and ask yourself what do you still do as an adult that you were taught as a kid? How have those habits affected you as an adult?

In this book, my goal is to help parents learn how to teach their children financial education at home. Many parents don't teach financial education because they don't know how. This book will help you get started. If you begin teaching your child at a young age the concept of "paying yourself first," which is putting money away specifically for building wealth, and how to put money into different types of accounts rather than just one (a practice called diversification), they will have a better chance of becoming wealthy. It is my hope that you will find the principles used throughout this book simple, clear, and doable.

We will explore eleven key principles that will help guide you in setting your child up for financial success. First, we will begin by going through characteristics you should possess as a financial parent. It is important for parents to teach about finances, so their children will have a chance to live the best life possible. Next, we will go through building your child's financial mindset. The younger you begin teaching your child about money the better your chances are to create a child who saves money out of habit. We will also go through the different conversations you should have with your child at every age. During each age level, parents should be helping their children grow in their financial knowledge.

Because it is important for you to be involved in helping to set your child up for financial success starting from birth, we will go over the different accounts you can open. It is important that you have more than one account open for your child to help diversify their funds. I will also go over the power of using compounding interest. Opening up accounts with compounding interest will help show your child how to make their money grow faster. I will also share a product that most people overlook that can help your child build wealth. You will see how its features can benefit your child the most.

After understanding what types of financial accounts are available for your children, you should help them choose products wisely. I will go over different taxes your children should be aware of and what financial products will best help them avoid paying unnecessary taxes. You will learn the three different tax categories the financial products fall into. You will also learn about the importance of building money-making assets. If anyone wants to have consistent income, it is smart to invest in long-term assets that can bring in residual income.

Once you have helped your child set up a strong financial foundation, it is important to teach them how to remain financially stable. I will talk about how to introduce your child to the concept of credit and how to avoid debt. Most children have no idea how their credit report can affect them as an adult until they find themselves in debt. I will also discuss why it is important for your child to engage in entrepreneurship. With the 2008 recession we experienced, it is important for children to learn how to stand on their own if they want to be able to maintain their wealth during challenging times. Lastly, I will discuss a simple system that can be used to help your child manage their money more effectively on a daily basis. Having a set way to handle money can save your child some time, energy, and money.

Even if you did not get the proper financial education growing up, this book will give you an opportunity to turn things around for your children. By learning and applying the principles in this book, your children will be informed and prepared to make better financial decisions. Being financially independent involves you making healthy money choices. The earlier you teach your children how to do the right things with their money, the more time they will have toward saving for their future. We can all agree that there are some financial habits that we learned from our parents we still use today. As parents, you hold the torch that helps light the path to a better financial future for your children. Now is the time to erase the habits that have put you into an unfavorable financial situation and begin to embrace the change of financial literacy in your household by enforcing financial parenting skills.

Mindset Building

Once your mind changes, everything on the outside will
change along with it. - Steve Maraboli

CHAPTER 1

Becoming A Financial Parent

Once you enter into the exciting world of parenthood, life as you know it changes. You are no longer responsible for only your well-being—you become responsible for your children's as well. For some, that is a scary thought, but it is reality. As a parent, you play a major role in helping shape your children's future habits.

It is up to parents to teach children the things they need to know in order to navigate throughout life. Because of the significant role parents play in their children's lives, children look to them as an example to follow. Starting as early as toddlers, they begin to repeat what parents do and say. That is why it is important for parents to remain aware of the behaviors they are teaching their children, consciously and subconsciously.

As children grow older, they take the information they learned from childhood to become independent in different areas of their lives. Many of them find themselves doing well in areas such as getting a job and taking care of their everyday duties; however, when it comes to managing money and saving for the future, they often find themselves struggling. This is because most children don't grow up in homes where parents intentionally teach financial skills. The majority of the financial habits children pick up from their parents are taught subconsciously.

There are several possible reasons parents choose not to talk to their children about finances. However one of the most common reasons this happens is because they didn't see it done to them when they were younger. Another reason is because many parents are not comfortable with their own financial situation, so they don't feel qualified to teach about finances. On the other hand, many parents who would love to help their children learn financial skills have obstacles when it comes to how to get started. As a result of parents delaying the process, many children find themselves in undesirable financial situations as adults.

In order to help children have the best financial life possible, parents must take action as early as possible. Parents must learn not only how to be great traditional parents, but they must learn how to be great financial parents at the same time. Financial parents understand that in order to help their children be successful in their finances, they have to change their own financial mindset first. They understand the importance of talking about money with their children even if their parents didn't talk to them. Rather than focusing on what they didn't learn as a child, they look for ways to make life better for their children. By doing so, their children develop habits that most children are never exposed to.

In this chapter, we will explore the seven S.U.C.C.E.S.S. principles that financial parents use to help their children. When it comes to their children, financial parents set expectations, unite with other financial parents, create financial plans, cultivate their gifts, encourage them through financial education, spend time with them, and set an example for them to follow. By following these principles, financial parents give their children a greater chance of having the best financial future possible.

In order to help you in your transition into financial parenting, it is a good idea for you to see where you stand with each principle. A good way to do this is to rate yourself on a scale of 1 to 5 (5 being the highest) on whether or not you are currently using each principle in your household. By doing so, you will be able to see what areas you are currently doing well in and what areas you can improve on.

The S.U.C.C.E.S.S. Principles

1 Set expectations about money.

Financial parents set expectations because they know expectations help set the bar for their children. Children of financial parents know upfront what their parents require of them. When they know what is required of them as early as possible, it is easier for them to incorporate those particular habits into their daily routine. It is also easier for children to remain focused.

When teaching their children about money, financial parents believe it is important to set realistic expectations. They set expectations for their children that are age appropriate. It is important to financial parents to be fair. Financial parents who have more than one kid believe in setting different expectations for each child. Because each child is distinct, they consider each child's strengths and weaknesses before they set standards for them.

In striving to be fair with their expectations, financial parents also believe in balance. They don't set expectations that are too high that will cause their children to become discouraged, nor too low that their children are not challenged enough. To help them keep a good balance, financial parents ask their children whether or not their expectations are reasonable. By doing so, their children feel a part of the decision-making process.

When children are a part of the decision-making process, they are more likely to want to meet their parents' expectations. Children are also more likely to succeed in meeting expectations when they are praised for their performance. Financial parents know the power of praising their children. They know that the more they praise their children, the better chance they will have of steering their children in the right financial direction.

To make goals appear more attainable for their children, financial parents help their children set short- and long-term financial goals. They focus on breaking up long-term goals by celebrating the short-term successes. For example, buying a car seems so far away for most children, but financial parents celebrate the short-term successes along the way. As children meet their financial milestones, the more willing they are to continue saving toward a bigger goal.

There are times when children will not always meet their goals. In those cases, financial parents encourage their children to continue working toward them. They teach their children the importance of never giving up. However, if their children continue to not reach their goals, they sit down with them and re-evaluate the goals. The goal of a financial parent is to gradually build their children's financial confidence by helping them achieve their goals.

2 Unite with others who have an interest in financial education.

Financial parents believe that you are a product of your environment, so it is important for them to connect with others who have a common interest in financial education. Because they know their children will follow in their footsteps, financial parents make it a priority to find different ways to increase their financial knowledge. They prefer to hang around individuals who can help build their financial mindset. Once they have built their financial mindset, they become more confident when it comes to helping their children build theirs.

As parents search for ways to build their financial mindset, they often attend different events such as seminars. These type of events give parents a chance to come into contact with other financial parents. For parents who are not able to attend events, they choose to read different articles or books. Some parents even go as far as getting a financial mentor. They feel having a mentor can help guide them by keeping them accountable for their financial habits.

Financial parents are dedicated to changing their habits. They know that the people they associate with will help dictate their success; that is why they put emphasis on defining their associations. They also know that it is important to monitor who their children associate with. Their children are often part of different organizations or community events that are specifically designed for teaching young people financial education. These environments help parents reinforce what they teach at home.

3 Create a financial plan.

Financial parents begin to prepare for their children's financial future before they are born. Both parents sit down and have a conversation about how they were taught about money as a child and discuss how they want to teach their children. By exploring their childhoods, they are able to analyze what information was beneficial and what else can be added. This helps both parents stay on the same path. After discussing what type of financial information they want to teach their children, financial parents write their goals down on paper. They believe if you don't write your goals down, you will find it hard to reach them. Most parents plan birthday parties, vacations, and other events weeks in advance, but they never really sit down and plan their children's financial future. Financial parents are not like most parents—they actually put together a visual financial plan

to help their children meet specific goals.

The plans parents create for their children are called financial road-maps. A financial roadmap is a long-term, visual financial plan that helps financial parents keep track of what direction they want to go in when it comes to teaching their children financial skills. The roadmap identifies the different financial conversations they want to have with their children at each age, and it lays out what types of accounts they will set up for them. These roadmaps are important to financial parents because they give them a clearer picture of how they want to incorporate financial parenting into their daily routine. We will talk more about roadmaps in chapter three.

Cultivate your children's gifts.

As soon as financial parents discover their children have talents, they begin cultivating them. By cultivating your children's talents, you help foster their growth. Financial parents see their children's talents and give them the opportunity and space to embrace them. Many of them allow their children to take lessons or be a part of an organization that will help them utilize their talents. Financial parents believe that the more they support their children by cultivating their talents, the more they will help their children succeed in their future endeavors.

Not only do financial parents want their children to succeed in mastering their talents, but they also want them to use their talents to have rewarding careers. They invest time in helping their children figure out what type of career they would like to have when they get older. They network and reach out to professionals in the field of study their children are interested in. They see if their children can do a "walk in my shoes" day. This is when a child spends maybe a day or a couple of hours with a professional to watch what they do. The experience will give children the opportunity to see if they really want to do that particular occupation before they waste two or four years in college in the wrong field of study. It also helps them begin planning for their future sooner.

5 Encourage your children to excel in life by using financial education.

Most parents don't think to incorporate financial education in their households. However, if you want to help prevent your children from making some of the same financial mistakes that you made as a young adult, it is important to incorporate some form of financial education. No matter what age your child is, there is something you can do to help them have a brighter financial future. The important thing is that you get started now.

To get the best results, financial parents teach their children financial concepts. When teaching their children concepts, they keep things simple. Sometimes parents can make things more complex than they need to be. Financial parents keep things simple because they don't want to turn their children off from learning things they really should know.

When it comes to teaching children different financial concepts, there are a number of ways to teach them. Financial parents use games such as Monopoly to help teach their children money-managing skills and how to plan ahead. The internet can also be a great resource when it comes to researching ways to teach your children financial skills. The main objective for financial parents is to find exciting ways to teach their children about finances that will keep them attentive.

Financial parents want their children to be able to enjoy the best life possible without worrying about how they will make ends meet. They start teaching their children about financial skills early because they believe in early prevention. They believe the more time their children have to practice a skill, the more successful they will be. They know that they are the key to helping their children build a strong financial foundation.

6 Spend time with your children.

Financial parents know the best way to get their children to do something is to have a good relationship with them. When children feel their parents genuinely care, they are more likely to exhibit positive behavior toward them. Sometimes parents get so caught up with their lives that they forget about helping their children be the best they can be. Financial parents believe when it comes to having a successful relationship with your children, you should invest in them mentally, physically, spiritually, and financially.

Many families no longer sit around the table together for dinner anymore. Financial parents use dinnertime as a time to talk to their children about different topics, such as money, and see how their day went. Showing an interest in what is going on with your children sends a clear message that they are important. Your children also feel like you value them when you allow them to express their opinions in a situation.

Financial parents also involve their children in financial decisions, using this additional time with their children as possible teachable moments. This not only creates confidence, but it makes your children feel like you take what they have to say into consideration. Many relationships between parents and their children struggle because children don't feel that they have a voice. Because children of financial parents feel comfortable talking to them, they have a chance to have a greater influence in all areas of their children's lives.

7 Set an example for your children to follow.

The saying "monkey see, monkey do" is often used when it comes to parents and their children. Financial parents work on setting a good example for their children to follow. They know that most behaviors that children exhibit are picked up from watching those who raised them. It is harder to teach your children positive financial habits if they don't see you doing them first. You have to be willing to work on changing your financial situation before you begin preaching to your children, or they may see you as a hypocrite.

Even if you don't feel you are handling your finances properly, you can still help your children. Showing your children how you have financial goals that you are working toward is just as important as already having great habits in place. Being perfect is not always the goal when it comes to setting an example for your children. Instead, having the conversation, being open, and showing your own effort is a valuable example.

Another thing important to financial parents is the home environment they create for their children. As we discussed in the beginning of the chapter, you have to be conscious of your actions when it comes to your children. Even if you become frustrated about your finances,

#gettingstartednow

you have to be aware of how you react in front of your children. Your children absorb the atmospheres they are placed in. This doesn't mean you can't express your feelings when faced with obstacles, but the way you handle them in front of your children should be considered. For example, if a child grows up in a home where there is love and support, it will be easier for them to show love toward others. Modeling is more effective when you want your children to do what you say.

Now that you have finished going through each principle, I want you to reflect on where you stand in your journey toward becoming a financial parent. Incorporating these principles in your household will help you have a smoother transition in becoming a financial parent. Some of you may feel you are already on track to becoming a great financial parent, while others may feel you have a long way to go. The great thing about the entire process is that it does not matter where you are, you just have to follow the system and you will eventually reach your destination.

After you have finished rating yourself on each principle, you should evaluate your areas of opportunity and begin to gradually incorporate them into your lifestyle. These are areas where you scored a three or below. You should continue your normal routine for the areas you scored well in. Now that you have made a personal decision to revamp your mindset and dedicate yourself to teaching your children financial skills, you are ready to help shape your children's financial mindset.

Shaping
The Right
Mindset

In life, our mindset will determine how far we go. According to Wikipedia, a mindset is a set of assumptions, methods, or notations held by one or more people or groups of people that is so established that it creates a powerful incentive within these people or groups to continue to adopt or accept prior behaviors, choices, or tools. It is a fixed state of mind. What we learn as children helps set our attitude about life. That is why it is important for parents to monitor what types of mindsets they are helping their children develop.

Many people don't think about how important it is to build their mindset with positive thoughts. You have to constantly fill your mind with positive thoughts daily. This can be done through reading daily affirmations or scriptures, joining inspirational morning conference calls, listening to positive music, listening to a positive public speaker on the radio or on a CD, watching an inspirational morning television show, and the list goes on. How you start your day will have an impact on your attitude for that day.

When you are trying to build healthy thoughts, you have to be careful

#mentalbankaccount

with what you allow yourself to be a part of. When you were young, your perspective about life was shaped by the environment you grew up in. This includes the people you allowed yourself to associate with. Associations are very important because they help define who we are and, eventually, who our children become.

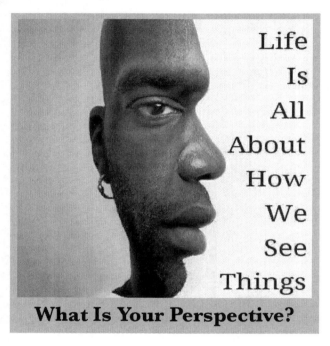

What Is Your Perspective?

As an adult, your perspective about life is formed by the environments you allow yourself to be a part of. Some of the people you hang around are reflective of the way of life you have conformed to. For example, if you constantly hang around negative people, you will find yourself falling into the same trap. The conversations you engage in with your friends begin to shape the way you look at the people and things in your life.

If your friends think they will never be rich, you will begin to think that you can't be rich because no one in your circle has money. Even if

#mentalbankaccount

you are presented with an opportunity to make more money by doing something extra on the side, you will have a hard time believing you can be successful because the people in your circle are not financially successful. Because you continue to hang around these types of people and never surround yourself with people who have a positive outlook about life and are making extra income for themselves, you never allow yourself to reach a higher level of living.

I want you to think about the people in your life who have had a major influence on you. Ask yourself what habits they possessed that you can see in yourself. If you really think about it, I am sure you can think of some of your negative habits and realize how that person rubbed off on you. Having a strong mindset is the key to a successful life beyond money.

How a Financial Mindset Is Formed

As a parent, one of the biggest duties you have is to help shape your child's mindset. What you allow your child to experience will have an overall effect on how they go about life. That's why it is important to make sure you are a positive influence.

We know that as a child starts learning to talk, they pick up on every little word. I watched a couple curse around their three-year-old daughter, and when she repeated it, they thought it was funny. Because that child grew up hearing her parents curse about everything, she thought it was okay for her to do the same. Her parents didn't realize that their habits had rubbed off on their child until she got upset one day as a teenager and decided to use profanity to express her feelings. They were in total shock!

When forming habits, kids pick up more from their parents than you can imagine. As they see something over and over again, they record it in their minds. That's why you have to keep in mind what lessons you may be unintentionally teaching your child. Not only do you have to watch what you do and say around your children, you have to watch what you allow them to spend their time doing.

Because we live in a society where the television and the Internet are raising children, it is a good idea for parents to monitor their children's habits. The average household has at least two televisions. When parents are not taking an active interest in what their children are watching, they begin to see changes in their household that they don't like. With YouTube and other phone apps, it is not uncommon for kids to watch inappropriate content. As parents, you have to use your available time to focus on your children. By establishing certain characteristics in your child at an early age, they are more likely to make better decisions when faced with adversities or temptations.

As you can see, a lot goes into helping set your child up for a bright future. The same goes for their financial future. You have to play an active role in teaching them how to be confident, how to be disciplined, how to set goals, and how to constantly build their mindset with positive thinking. It is true that what you teach a child while they are young, they will carry with them throughout life. To get your child where they need to be financially, you have to decide to take an active interest in their financial future.

As you begin shaping your children's mental bank account which is their mindset about money, you should begin by setting the expec-

#mentalbankaccount

tation that they become a super saver. A super saver is someone who has a mindset that focuses on delayed gratification. They focus on not spending money for an immediate reward, but rather waiting till later to receive a bigger reward. They realize the importance of putting money away for all the things they need in the future such as a car, a house, college, and retirement.

The first thing you should do in helping your child become a super saver is to help them understand how super savers look at money. Many children fail at becoming financially independent because they never understand how to handle their money. The younger your child learns the habits of a super saver, the better chance they have to become wealthy. Let's look at how super savers view their money.

The Habits of Super Savers

1 Super savers value their money.

Most people don't think twice before they spend their money, especially children. That is why it is important to shape your child's super-saver mindset to value money early. When your child values money, they understand that it is used as a resource to help them reach their financial goals.

They understand that money is not something you spend only on your wants and needs, but it can also lead to multiple streams of income if it is used properly. Super savers are taught early how to control all of their money.

2   Super savers earn their money.

When super savers have their own money, they become more engaged when it comes to making financial decisions. They begin to think about the benefits of the things they buy. Earning their own money also allows super savers to grow their money faster. They don't have to wait for special occasions or their parents in order to receive monetary gifts. Allowing your child to gain hands-on experience with money will also improve your chances of helping them become financially independent.

3   Super savers manage their money.

There are people all around you who make money, but they are still living from check to check because they don't manage their money properly. That is why it is so important to incorporate financial education. It is not enough to just earn money. Parents of super savers teach their children how they should handle their money. They teach their children how to diversify their money by putting it into different types of financial accounts. Having different accounts allow super savers the opportunity to save more money by determining which accounts they will be able to take money from and those they will not take money from.

4   Super savers spend their money wisely.

When it comes to spending money, we have to start teaching our kids smart spending habits. Many Americans struggle financially because they try to live above their means. Average people spend all their hard-earned money trying to buy things to impress people who don't even care about them. Most rich people stay wealthy

#mentalbankaccount

by living average lifestyles, not by flaunting their wealth. When the housing crisis took place in 2007, many homes went into foreclosure because a lot of people were in loans they couldn't afford. People's priorities were mixed up. They focused more on impressing others instead of being debt free. It is important that you help your child stay focused and on the right track to help prevent them from making poor spending decisions.

5 Super savers save their money.

Super savers save money with an end result in mind. When you save money, you don't have to live worrying how you are going to fix things if something happens. Saving money not only helps you build wealth for yourself, but it also gives you a peace of mind. The earlier your child understands the importance of saving, the better off they will be when they become an adult.

When building a super-saver mindset, you have to help your child see the benefits of saving. That is why when your child is young, you should not just buy them everything they ask for. Some things your child should help pay for. Even if they put in 35 cents when they are five to buy an item, they are still better off than not contributing anything. When you ask your children to contribute to their purchases, they will be more reluctant to spend their money because they know they have a financial responsibility. The goal in the early years is not about your child contributing a lot of money, but rather helping them get into the habit of wanting to save.

6 Super savers share their money.

By giving back, super savers build their humility and understand they have a moral obligation to the world. The earlier parents expect their children to contribute to others, the easier it will be for them to share their money as adults. Even if your child does not have money to give, they can still invest their time toward helping others. Investing time in helping others who are less fortunate teaches children how to be more grateful for the things they have. They begin to have an attitude of gratitude where they appreciate the little things in life that go beyond just having money.

7 Super savers invest their money.

During the course of their childhood, many children collect a large amount of money. Starting from the baby shower, some children begin receiving monetary gifts. Unfortunately, some parents don't help the child use the money toward a good cause. Instead of helping their children make better decisions on how to use the money, many parents will allow the child to decide how to use it.

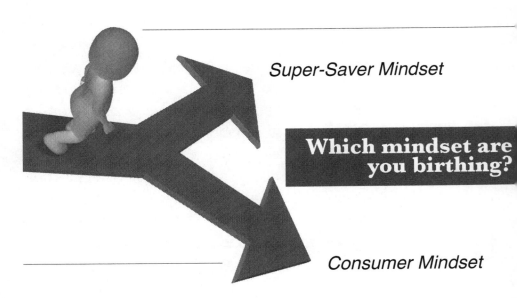

Super-Saver Mindset

Which mindset are you birthing?

Consumer Mindset

It is the parents' responsibility to be instrumental in helping their child diversify their money and not spend it in one place. Children get excited about receiving money and immediately begin to plan what they will buy with it. There should be a system in place to help distribute the funds. Having a system helps your child stay consistent with their spending habits.

If your children grow up with the mentality that they have to save, it makes it much easier for them to become disciplined in their finances. Habits are triggered in our brains, they become routines, and the brain begins to repeat the habits because it gives the brain an incentive to remember. Once a child has money, they should begin investing their money in accounts that will give them compounding interest. The more money they invest, the better chance they have of becoming financially independent.

For children to succeed financially, we have to help mold them. Even if your child hasn't started saving yet, knowing the habits of a super saver will help put them on the right track. The sooner you teach your child about good saving habits, the earlier you will be able to nip bad habits in the bud. Not teaching your children these seven habits of a super saver could lead them to believe you are their walking ATM that will give them money any time they see something they want. If you are not building a strong financial foundation for your children to follow, it will be easy for them to fall into the consumer mindset where they focus on their immediate wants without thinking about the consequences. It also involves your child spending all their money on materialistic items and you being receptive to it. As soon as your child sees that you allow this type of behavior, the mentality is born. When you are not encouraging your children

#mentalbankaccount

to save, it is easy for them to get caught up with impulse buying. Impulse buying involves buying things that are unplanned. Have you ever gone into a store planning to buy two items, but ending up with ten? People are usually attracted to items that have a great marketing message. The majority of people purchase items based on their emotions or feelings. There continues to be a growing problem in the US today of most people not knowing how to turn off their consumer mentality because they were never required to save while growing up.

A 2011 survey of parents and teens from Capitol One found that only 57 percent of parents surveyed had discussed the difference between a want and a need.[4] Many kids get into a bad habit of throwing things in the shopping cart just because they want it. With so many commercials targeting young people, it can be hard for them to understand that they really don't have to have everything they see on television. Your child only knows right from wrong when you teach them. Getting your child in the habit of creating a list before they go to the store and sticking with it is a great way to cut down on impulse buying. Another way to help cut down on impulse buying is to get them in the habit of carrying a set amount of money into the store. It is important to monitor your child's spending habits closely. Having them write down and analyze their expenses helps you track how their money is being spent. It also allows you to adjust your parenting to address your child's changing financial perspectives.

The only way for your child to become a great super saver is to practice. Practicing the habits of a super saver will help with their discipline. You should be incorporating activities into their routine that encourage them to save. Some parents accomplish this by helping their

[4] http://phx.corporate-ir.net/phoenix.zhtml?c=70667&p=irol-newsArticle&ID=1596344&highlight

#mentalbankaccount

children set goals and match their children's contributions. When you give your children incentives, they are more reluctant to save.

The goal is to start teaching your child as early as two years old the concept of saving, the concept of being their own person, and the concept of not putting all of their money toward one item. Because children are ready to learn by nature, it is easier to help shape their mindset at an early age. If you never encourage your child to take on the habits of a super saver while they are young, it will be more challenging for them to form the habits as an adult. That's why it is important to help steer your child in the right direction.

When it comes to birthing a financial mindset, your child will either grow up with a super-saver mindset or a consumer mindset. You help control which one your child develops. Teaching them how money works will help them build smart money habits. As you set expectations for your child to become a super saver in the beginning, they will become better equipped for their future.

3

Conversations at Every Level

When most women get the news that they are expecting a baby, they immediately start preparing for the baby's arrival. They begin eating healthier foods, taking vitamins, and engaging in less stressful activities. Their main objective is to make sure they birth a healthy baby. Once the baby is born, parents focus on helping their child progress through each stage of development.

In the early years, parents feed their children with a bottle and gradually progress into feeding them solid food. When parents feed their children, they are teaching them how to eat so they can eventually feed themselves. Parents also teach their children how to gradually go from crawling to walking to help them gain more independence. As children begin walking and become familiar with their surroundings, most parents start to prepare their children's brain for language and the alphabet by reading to them. During each phase, children are able to successfully progress to the next one because of the guidance they receive from their parents.

#talkaboutmoney

Financial parenting is similar to traditional parenting. Financial parents are responsible for teaching their children the skills needed to help them progress in their financial development. Children should be gradually increasing their financial understanding as they go through each phase. It is important to take baby steps with them in their first years as their brains are developing. Your conversations about money should be very basic to help motivate them. The more technical parents are, the more disinterested their children will become.

After watching several parents and their relationships with their children around money over the years, I became very disappointed with the way the parents were allowing their children to handle money. Many of the children received a great amount of money from birthday parties, from allowances, and from making good grades, but they were never required to save any of it. It was during this time that I realized a need for a program to help parents teach their children how to better manage their finances. That's when I devised the Financial Head Start Program, a program designed to help give parents insight into the different phases that are key to a child's financial development.

The Financial Head Start Program is divided into five phases: the planning phase, the foundation phase, the independent phase, the transitioning phase, and the coaching phase. Each area focuses on parents instilling the right financial principles during a specific age range. It is important to remember that every child learns at a different rate, so it is up to the parents to determine the speed at which they will teach their children. Let's look at what should be taking place during each stage.

#talkaboutmoney

The Planning Phase

The planning phase is the first phase and the one that is often over-looked. Many parents know the cost that can come with having a child, but very few of them begin planning for their child's financial future before they are born. It is very common for adults to plan birth-day parties, weddings, vacations, and many other things months in advance, so why is it that many parents are not putting a plan together for their children's financial future? If you ask me, I don't believe society puts enough emphasis on the importance of doing so. This is the stage where parents should focus on putting together a long-term financial plan to help ensure that their kids have the best financial outcome.

As you learned earlier, a financial roadmap is one of the best ways to create a financial plan. It helps parents stay on track with all the financial goals they want to help their children achieve. When mak-ing a roadmap, all you will need is a piece of paper, something to write with, and your ideas. The roadmap doesn't have to be fancy unless you want it to be.

Creating A Financial Roadmap

To start your roadmap, you begin by drawing a line down the center of your paper. Label one side "Financial Education" and the other side "Financial Accounts." Under the financial education column, begin by brainstorming all the financial concepts you want to teach your children. As we go through the rest of the phases, you will get a better idea of what financial information is important for kids to learn.

After you have completed the financial education column, you are ready to move to the financial accounts column. You will begin this section by brainstorming what types of financial accounts you want to open up for your child. The three most common types of accounts for children are scheduled accounts, emergency accounts, and fun accounts. A scheduled account is a long-term interest account set up to help fund children's specific needs in the future. An emergency account is an account set up to handle children's short-term needs. A fun account is an extra account parents have for their children just because. This account may be an extra savings or scheduled account.

In the next chapter, you will have a chance to see different types of financial products you may consider using to establish these accounts. No matter what your reasons may be for saving, you should find the right products that fit what you are looking to do for your child. If you and your spouse are not sure about what types of financial products to purchase, you may choose to schedule an appointment with a financial professional.

When you have a financial plan in place, it helps make things easier for you. It gives you a guide to follow to make sure you went over everything you planned to cover. As you continue to go through the different phases, there may be special situations where you may have to slow down or go back over things from previous stages, based on your child's progression. With that in mind, you should be constantly evaluating your child's progress and making adjustments to your plan accordingly.

The Foundation Phase

When you think about the word foundation, what thoughts imme-diately come to mind? For me, I think about the start of something. When it comes to financial development, the foundation phase is where parents start helping their children understand the funda-mentals of money. The things parents teach their children from two years old to six years old will have the greatest impact on the finan-cial decisions they make as they get older. Let's look at what hap-pens during the age ranges within this phase.

1 month – 3 years old

When a child is between these ages, parents should begin opening the financial accounts they listed on their child's financial roadmap. By setting up accounts now, the money placed in them will have more time to grow. Time plays a major factor when it comes to help-ing kids build financial stability. When parents open up accounts now, their children have a higher chance of having a prosperous future.

Parents get to pick and choose which accounts they want for their children. For example, one couple may decide they want to open up two scheduled accounts for their child. One account may be for funding college while the other account is for building wealth. Then they may decide they want to open up an emergency account and a fun account later on.

By having an emergency account, parents can begin saving money toward any unexpected circumstances that may come up. Using a fun account as a savings account allows parents the opportunity to use the account to fund whatever their child needs as they grow. It could be used to pay for things such as diapers, clothing, daycare, and recreational activities. Parents would also have an opportunity to keep more money in their personal accounts by having these designated accounts in place.

As children get closer to three years old, parents should begin introducing them to financial principles. A good concept to start with is how to "pay yourself first." This is when money is set aside to help build your financial future. This is important for kids to understand now. It becomes harder for most people as they get older because they tend to get more consumed with using their money to buy things and to take care of their responsibilities. Learning how to do this at an early age gives kids a chance to practice the habit over and over again until it becomes natural for them to do it.

A great way to help children get accustomed to following this principle is by having them store their money in a piggybank or a savings jar. Either way parents choose is fine; however, I will be referring to a piggybank throughout this book. As parents begin to introduce their child to what a piggybank is and what they will be using it for, it is important for them to have money already stored in it and to demonstrate how to use it. By doing so, they are leading by example.

When talking to my friend John about his childhood, he told me he remembered when his grandfather bought him a piggybank and taught him how to use it. He was so excited about finding coins to put in the bank. He stated that using a piggybank was the main thing he remembered from his childhood about saving. As a result, he still saves in his piggybank nineteen years later.

As we see in this example, it is important for parents to be intentional when it comes to teaching their children financial habits. The majority of the behaviors children display throughout their lifetime are learned behaviors, things they have picked up from their circle of influence. As a parent, it is important that you model the behaviors that will help steer your child in the right financial direction.

4 – 6 years old

As children reach this age range, parents should begin helping them increase their knowledge about money. This includes teaching them what money is, how to identify it, how to distinguish between a want and a need, how to set financial goals, and how to share money with others for a good cause. Teaching these principles now helps give your child a strong financial start that they can build on.

As you begin teaching your child how to identify coins and bills, the money stored in the piggybank will be great to use. Another option for parents who prefer not to use real money with their children is to use play money instead. Both methods are effective because they allow kids to follow along with what you are saying. It is also a good time for parents to go over how coins and bills are equivalent to each other since most kids are learning to count. This will also help your child get a jumpstart on their math skills.

As you engage in activities with your children, to be the most effective, you should be sure they are relevant to the concept you are teaching. The more hands-on opportunities that children are presented with, the easier it will be for them to retain the information they learn. A good way for parents to monitor whether or not their children are catching on to what they are teaching is to watch their body language. It is also important to reward your child as they begin to understand what you are teaching them. Being excited and rewarding your children are two ways to help you get your point across to children, especially those in this age range.

#talkaboutmoney

After introducing what money looks like to your child, you should move on to helping them understand that money is used as a medium of exchange. This is a time to explain the difference between a want and a need. Discussing the basic needs, such as food, shelter, clothing, and transportation, will help your child see the importance of these things in their life. A good way to help your child begin distinguishing between a want and a need is to role-play with them.

You may choose to set some items around the house and have your child pretend they are at a store or take them to an actual store. Children should be able to pick out the items they want and discuss why they chose each item and what category the item fits into. Another way you may accomplish this is by using magazines and allowing them to cut out pictures for each category. The objective is to keep things fun for your child and teach them a lesson at the same time.

Another thing children should learn how to do is share their money and time with others. This may take the form of giving to a charity, tithing at church, tipping a waiter, volunteering at a local shelter, or giving to other special causes. Each month, week, or year, you should let your child make a contribution with you, no matter how small it may be, or volunteer with you. This will help build their desire to want to give to others.

Children should also learn how to go about setting financial goals early. When your child has something they are aiming for, they are more likely to stay disciplined and try to reach the goal. They should learn how to distinguish between short- and long-term financial goals. Short-term goals are things you would like to reach within a five year time frame. Long-term goals are goals that go past five years.

#talkaboutmoney

When helping children understand the difference between the two types of goals, something as simple as writing down items on a piece of paper, cutting them out, and putting them in a container to draw out of can be beneficial. For example, going to college, buying a car, and purchasing a house are some things you can put in the container to represent long-term goals. To express short-term goals, you could use things such as a toy or lunch money. As children pick the items out, parents should see what items they chose and ask them questions such as how long they think it will take for them to reach the goal and why.

Making your children have conversations with you about the financial skills you are teaching them helps you make sure they understand what you are saying and makes things more interactive. It is important to listen to what your children have to say so they will be empowered to learn more because they feel valued. As children know what money is, how to identify it, how it is used, how to set financial goals, and how to give to others, they are more likely to be confident in the financial decisions they make. The earlier that children learn these principles, the stronger their financial foundation will be. Let's move on to the next phase.

The Independent Phase

As many children get older, they desire to do things on their own. The independent stage is where parents should begin teaching their children how to handle their own finances. Teaching them things—such as how to earn money, how to manage money, how to store money in financial institutions, and how to budget—can help children get on the right financial path. Let's look at how these things are accomplished in each age level.

#talkaboutmoney

7 – 9 years old

By the time most children reach these ages, they begin to get settled in their ways. They also become more aware of how their parents are handling finances, so it is important to continue to be a great role model for them. Teaching your child about money is just like telling your infant "no" when they are trying to put things in their mouth. After you say "no" several times, they eventually begin to follow your commands and stop what they were doing.

The same behavior goes with teaching your child how to save early. The more conversations you have about saving, the easier it will become for your child to handle their money properly. As you are encouraging your child to save, you should also make sure they understand why you have them doing certain things. This also helps you reinforce the habits your child may be struggling with.

In order to help children save money, parents should allow them to begin earning income. By doing so, children are able to further their money-management skills. One way parents can help their children is by giving them an allowance. Many parents have different views on whether or not they should give an allowance. If you are not comfortable with the idea of giving your child money for doing chores, you may choose to pay them a base allowance for their performance in school or other side jobs they do.

The other alternative is to teach them how to become an entrepreneur. An entrepreneur is someone who provides a service or sells a product to earn a profit. When your child is an entrepreneur, they not only build their leadership skills, but they are also able to learn how to become independent faster. Parents should help guide their children but allow them to make their own choices. As they are able to make their own decisions, children are able to work on their decision-making skills.

Learning entrepreneurial skills at this age allows your child to reach their financial goals faster. Whichever method you decide to choose is based on your personal choice. I see both sides; however, I do believe parents should give kids a set amount of money weekly, monthly, or quarterly to help them understand how to handle money properly even if they don't believe in allowance or helping their child become an entrepreneur.

As children are making money, they should learn the importance of diversifying their money. Practicing diversification allows children to see how they should save their money in more than one place. A good way to teach this concept is by incorporating a spending jar in addition to your child saving in their piggybank.

A spending jar is used to help your child begin saving toward short-term things they want to do or purchases they would like to make. The jar benefits both parents and children. It keeps your children interested in wanting to save because they are able to buy things. Parents benefit from the jar because they are able to keep things simple when explaining how to place money in more than one place for different reasons.

After your child has a basic understanding of the importance of storing things in different places, you should begin to talk to them about different financial institutions to help them get a better understanding of how things operate in the real world. Because experiences are one of the best ways for children to learn, taking your child on a trip to a bank or credit union gives them an opportunity to see things for themselves.

#talkaboutmoney

Before you take your child to a bank or credit union, you may want to go over some basic financial terminology that they may hear. This will help them understand what is going on before you arrive. It is also good for your child to go back over the terms you taught them when they get to the financial institution and get any questions they may have answered. Here is a list of some of the terms you may want to go over:

Financial Goals
Goals you write down to help you set a reasonable expectation about the amount of money you are willing to save each week, month, or year.

Pay Yourself First
(This is a good time to go back over the importance of this concept) When you pay yourself first, you put money away in a specific account to help build a strong financial future.

Personal Finance
How individuals choose to manage their money.

Bank
A financial institution where you keep your money so that it is safe and you can take money out of your account when you need it.

Credit Union
They work similarly to a bank; however, you have to be a member to use it.

Account
An account is a place where you store your money when you leave it at the bank or credit union.

Account Number
A number that the bank or credit union gives you to identify your account.

Deposit
When you add money to your account.

Deposit Slip
The form you complete when you are going to add money to

your account at a bank or credit union.

Withdrawal
When you take money out of your account.

Balance
Your balance is how much money you have after subtracting or adding money to your account.

Teller
The person at the bank or credit union who works behind the front counter and helps you with anything you need concerning your account.

ATM
A place located at a bank or credit union where you can go to get cash out of your account or make a deposit.

Overdraft
When you spend more money than you have available in your account.

Bank Statement
Sheets of paper, which normally come out monthly, that show you the beginning balance in your account during the previous month, the money that came out of your account through transactions, and your remaining balance.

Financial Advisor
A person who helps you pick out specific financial products to help you receive the most growth on your money.

Debit Card
This card is linked to your account at a bank or a credit union. It allows you to make a payment for something without using cash.

Prepaid Card
A card that allows you to only use the amount of money you deposited on the card.

As you go over debit cards and prepaid cards, it is more effective if you let your child see you as you are making a transaction and explain what you are doing. This will help them understand that these cards already have money on them and they are not a magic piece of plastic. It is also helpful to let your child see what a bank statement looks like. This will help them keep things in perspective as they see how some of the terms you teach are listed on the statement.

The terms listed are essential to helping your child become familiar with financial institutions. Remember: If your child is more advanced, you may decide to teach more things. The goal is to give your child some basic knowledge beforehand so they don't feel clueless when they go on their visit. When children have a better understanding of things, they are able to enjoy the experience more.

On their trip, children should be able to deposit money from their piggybank into an account. The account may be one already established by the parents, or the parents may want to let their child be a part of setting up a savings account. Whichever way you choose, you should explain what you are doing and why it is important. Once the deposit is completed, you should make sure you show your child the amount you deposited or the amount you have in the actual account. This will help encourage your child to stay empowered and motivate them to continue saving.

Another concept children should become familiar with at this time is how to make a budget, also known as a financial blueprint. A budget gives you an estimated amount of income that you will have on a monthly basis to take care of your wants and needs. It is also a great tool to help children stay on track with their spending habits. By helping your child see how their money is being spent and how much they are able to put toward other things such as saving, you are helping them learn how to manage their money better.

#talkaboutmoney

During this age level, your child's budget should include a set amount that you allow them to spend each month toward what they want, and it should also include how much they will be saving each month. If your child is running their own business and they have to buy things, you would want to include those things on the list as well. As your child gets older, the things they put on their budgets will get longer as they begin taking care of more responsibilities. Allowing your child to make money mistakes now gives you an opportunity to help correct their habits before they become adults.

When going over a budget, it is necessary to go over the concept of "living within your means." People who do this are cautious not to spend more money than they have available. A good way to help your child practice this concept, aside from creating a budget, is to have your child record their spending habits in a journal. This will help both of you keep track of their spending habits and see what they spend most of their money on. Teaching this habit now will help give you a better grip on how your child spends money before they become a teenager.

It is also vital to discuss how advertising and peer pressure can have a negative effect on your children's spending habits. As children grow, they tend to want to be like others rather than being themselves. This is a good time to share your personal story about some of the obstacles you faced at this age. If you have these types of discussions early and your children see how you overcame your obstacles, they will be better prepared to face theirs.

Some ways to help your children get into the habit of living within their means is by introducing them to comparison shopping and alternative shopping. Comparison shopping is when you pick an item you want and shop around for the best price. Let's say you saw a pair of shoes you fell in love with. Before you made the purchase, you would check around in different stores to see who has the lowest price before you bought the shoes.

Using alternative shopping methods mean you purposely shop at places with the lowest prices. Many people choose to make purchases online instead of a retail store because they can often find better deals. Places such as thrift stores are also popular places people choose to shop because of their low prices. Other good habits to teach children are how to use coupons and how to make purchases only when things go on sale. Learning these methods can help your child use the money they get in the future to their advantage.

10 – 12 years old

By the time children are between these ages, they should begin planning their career paths. Researching different occupations now will give children an opportunity to explore what types of careers are out there. A great way to help children to get a better understanding about the things people in their desired field of choice do on a daily basis is for parents to arrange a "walk in my shoes day." As I discussed earlier, this is a day where children are given the opportunity to shadow a professional and learn what they do.

Giving children the chance to connect with professionals now could possibly help lead them to a job in the future. This is important in this day and time, considering many people get hired based on who they know rather than their background experiences. Spending time with professionals now also allows children to explore different careers ahead of time, which can help cut down on the amount of time they waste in college being undecided on a field of study.

Planning ahead benefits parents by allowing them to waste less time saving for college if their child is interested in doing something that doesn't require a college education. On the other hand, if a child is interested in an occupation that requires them to have a degree or they just want to attend, this is a great age range to begin getting information about potential schools. This helps your child see how much money is needed in advance to attend the university. When you get children prepared ahead of time for the expectations of college, they are more likely to stay motivated to keep their grades up, and they will have a chance to qualify for different scholarships and grants.

Placing children in different organizations that help develop their career and leadership skills can also be beneficial. Parents who allowed their children to partake in entrepreneurial skills in the last age group should continue nurturing their children's dreams and invest in them if that is something they would like to continue to do as they get older. Finding your child a business owner to help mentor them if you are not one yourself is a great way to help increase their knowledge about running their own business. When parents support their children, they are more likely to stay focused and accomplish their dreams.

When children have a set career path in mind for their future, they are able to make more money faster. For example, if a child knows what career path they want to take, they have a chance to graduate college sooner and begin making money faster. Parents could also miss an opportunity to focus on building their child's entrepreneurial skills if they don't have an idea of what career direction their children would like to take. This could cause their children to miss out on making more income for themselves at a younger age.

Another way to set children up for the best future possible is to teach them how to make their money work for them by explaining what interest is and how it can affect their money. Interest is a percentage of money earned on top of the money invested; it is paid as an incentive to keep your money with a financial institution. There are two types of interest: simple and compounding. Later in the book, I will go more in detail about both types. When teaching about interest, it is best to keep things as simple as possible to help your child understand what is actually taking place.

A good way to teach your child how interest works is by giving them a dime on top of every dollar saved at the end of each month. It is a good idea to separate the money so your child will be able to see

Financial Education

Financial Accounts

BOTH ARE NECESSARY FOR FINANCIAL SUCCESS

#talkaboutmoney

the visual impact of the coins. After about six months, pull the dimes out and show them how the dimes helped their money grow. Going over how the dimes increase your child's money will help lead you into explaining the Rule of 72 and how it will help them build wealth faster in the future.

The Rule of 72 is a mathematical formula created by Albert Einstein that takes the number 72 and divides it by the interest rate to show you how many years it would take for your money to double. This is a concept that will help your children see the positive and negative side of interest. The formula will also help you when you begin to talk about managing debt and buying a car. Pulling out a statement from the scheduled account you opened up for your child in the foundation phase and showing them how the money has been growing through interest is a great way to help your child see a real-life scenario.

In the independent stage, parents are dedicated to giving children the proper education they will need to be able to go out and do things on their own. As children learn the importance of diversifying their money, storing it in financial institutions, budgeting, and using the Rule of 72, they are able to understand how to position themselves in order to have the most financial growth. In addition, when children know what they want to do ahead of time, they are able to make the necessary preparations to lead to the best result.

The Transitioning Phase

In this phase, parents continue to help their children become independent by teaching them principles that will help them transition into becoming an adult. Things taught during this time are workplace success habits, different types of financial accounts, paying taxes, paying bills, understanding different types of insurance, planning for retirement, and building credit. During the ages in this stage, parents tend to expect more from their children. They are expected to perform at their best and be able to apply all they have learned from the previous phases.

13 – 15 years old

As children enter this age range, it is appropriate for parents to begin preparing them for things they will possibly experience as adults. If your child would like to have a job rather than owning their own business, then this is the time to go over workplace success habits, also known as job skills. You should focus on explaining the ins and outs of working for someone.

Going through the process of seeking employment with your children is a good place to start. Children should learn how to go about looking for a job. Using resources such as online job ads or ads listed in a newspaper are good ways to help show children how employers go about finding potential employees. Another thing to discuss with children is what a résumé looks like and how to use it. The internet has many different sites to help you.

Because many kids begin working at the age of sixteen, it is necessary to teach them how to conduct themselves during an interview. Most young people don't know what they should and should not be doing at an interview. The best way to help your child excel in developing interviewing skills is for you to teach them. Going over things such as how to dress properly, how to answer questions, how to enter and leave the room, and how to follow up with employers will benefit your child greatly.

Using sites such as YouTube to help assist you with teaching your children these skills is a good idea. It is also good to encourage children to take a public speaking class to help them build up their confidence, which will make it easier for them to talk with future employers. When children are prepared ahead of time about what to expect when seeking employment, it helps lessen their stress. As a result, they have a greater chance of being considered for a position because they will be able to come across as a polished candidate. As children are learning about job skills, parents should also focus on helping them understand how to read a paycheck and introduce them to who the Internal Revenue Service (IRS) is and how different types of taxes will be taken out of their checks. On a typical paycheck, there are four automatic tax deductions unless you claim exempt. Those are federal taxes, state taxes, social security taxes, and Medicare taxes. You will learn more about what these taxes are when you get to the chapter on taxes.

Once your child receives their first paycheck, they should know how to manage it. That is why it is important for parents to go over different places to store money with their children. Describing different financial accounts to children will help give them an understanding about how each one is different. Some of the accounts to go over are checking accounts, savings accounts, certificates of deposit (CDs), money-market accounts, mutual funds, stocks, treasury accounts, and cash-value life insurance. Let's look at what each of these is:

Checking Account
A checking account is an account that you have with either a bank or a credit union where you have the opportunity to write a check or use a debit card to make transactions instead of using cash.

Savings Account

We talked about this in the earlier stages, but it is a good idea to go back over it. It is an account at a bank or credit union where you can safely store your money. These accounts usually give you an opportunity to gain a small amount of interest on your money.

Certificate of Deposit (CD)

When you open a CD, you are putting a set amount of money away for a set number of years. You are not able to touch the money until the set period has ended or you will be penalized.

Money-Market Account

A money-market account is a savings and an investment account. They require you to maintain a certain amount of funds in your account. They are similar to regular saving accounts because they allow you to have check-writing and money-transferring privileges.

US Treasury Accounts

US Treasury securities—such as bills, notes, and bonds— are debt obligations of the US government. When you buy a US Treasury security, you are lending money to the federal government for a specified period of time with a promise to gain a certain amount of interest.

Bonds

You become a creditor when you purchase a bond because you are lending money to a company in return for interest on the maturity date.

Stocks

When you invest in a stock, you become a shareholder, meaning you have ownership in a company's assets and earnings. You have invested in the company's performance.

Mutual Funds

These are a portfolio of different stocks you have invested in based on your risk tolerance.

Cash-Value Life Insurance

A set account in a life insurance product where you have a chance to gain interest on your money.

#talkaboutmoney

Sharing about different financial products now will help your child begin thinking about what products they would like to use to help manage their funds. This is not a time to make things complex, but rather a time to make sure your child understands what exists in the financial arena. The earlier you help your child understand what types of products exist, the sooner you can help them get started investing their own money. If your child wants to learn more about a specific account, you should book an appointment with a financial professional to help give them more information.

16 – 18 years old

These are the ages where you want to go back over any principles you feel you need to review. Your child should be able to comprehend and apply the financial concepts they have been taught up until now. Parents should focus on making their children's transition into adulthood as smooth as possible. They should inform their children about the different responsibilities they may have to take care of as adults.

As children grow up and move out on their own, they will need to decide whether they want to rent or buy a place to stay. Most children rent a place. Renting is very popular for many reasons. Some people like renting because someone else is responsible for fixing any problems that occur during their lease. I have listed some terms your child should become familiar with that will help give them a better understanding as they go through the process.

> **Renting**
> When you do not have ownership of a property. You sign a lease, which is an agreement about how long you will live on the property. Your landlord handles problems that you have with the property.

#talkaboutmoney

Lease
A contract you sign when renting that states the specifics about your stay, such as when you have to move out or renew your contract.

Buying
When you buy your own home or condo and have full ownership, you carry the responsibility of taking care of any repairs needed.

Rent-to-Own
The option to purchase a place that you are renting at some point during the contract.

Mortgage
The amount owed on your loan for a home that you pay back monthly.

These are a few terms to help your child get acquainted with their options as they leave home. Next, parents should introduce their child to what bills are and help them understand different types of insurance. This helps children realize that they will soon have to take over and do the things their parents are already taking care of for them. Allowing your child to be around you as you pay your bills is a good way to help them see how things work. Let's look at some terms you can use when you are explaining these things.

Finances
The name given to your financial obligations.

Utilities
Bills that you pay every month, such as your light bill and water bill.

Car Note
The amount of money you will pay monthly after purchasing a car.

Premium
Your monthly payment after purchasing insurance.

Grace Period
The amount of days an insurance company gives you before they cancel your policy for nonpayment.

Auto Insurance
This type of insurance, also known as car insurance, is needed in order to protect yourself while driving your car on the road.

Renter Insurance
This insurance will help cover the personal belongings in your house or apartment if you are renting from a landlord. It will also help fix any damages that may occur to the property that are your fault.

Homeowner Insurance
This type of insurance also covers your personal belongings and helps repair damages to the home. It also allows you to rebuild your home in case of a fire or natural disaster.

Personal Articles Insurance
If you have a valuable asset such as a wedding ring, a piece of art, or anything else of value, you can write a separate policy to help cover if something were to happen to it.

Health Insurance
This type of insurance helps cover any medical expenses that may occur, including doctor visits, emergency room visits and it also covers prescription drugs.

Dental Insurance
Covers your visits to a professional for dental care.

Vision Insurance
Insurance that helps you take care of your eyes.

Disability Insurance
Insurance that you may purchase to help take care of you when you become disabled and are not able to go to work. It helps give you a source of income.

Long-Term Care Insurance
This type of insurance is needed to take care of medical expenses when you are older and may not meet the qualifications of a government program. You are able to have money

available to hire someone to help take care of you or help fund your nursing home stay.

Life Insurance
Insurance you purchase to help pay funeral expenses and help provide income to your family in the event you were to pass away. It can also be used as a supplement to retirement or as extra savings. I will discuss more about this later.

These terms help your child have a better idea about the different things they may have to pay as an adult. It also helps them become familiar with the insurance industry. There are several other terms associated with these different types of insurance. You may choose to teach your child some of the terms or wait until they purchase a specific type of insurance and let the insurance professional go over the terms they need to know.

It is also necessary to begin talking about what credit is and how it can affect your child. The earlier they understand that they need to uphold good credit, the better the chances of them doing so. We will discuss later different habits you should begin to instill in your children to help prevent them from living in debt. Let's look at some key terms about credit you should go over with your child:

Credit Report
A report that reflects your financial history with different companies.

Credit Score
A number that determines whether or not a financial institution will extend credit to you or allow you to finance a loan. There are three credit bureaus that keep your credit score. They are Experian, TransUnion, and Equifax.

Loan
A certain amount of money you borrow. In return, you pay it back with interest.

Debt
   Money owed toward a financial obligation.
Financing
   When you receive money upfront for a loan or a purchase
   such as a car and sign an agreement to pay the money
   back under set terms.
Charge Card
   This is similar to a credit card; however, the cardholder is
   obligated to repay the debt to the card issuer in full by the
   due date, usually on a monthly basis, or be subject to late
   fees and restrictions on further card use.
Secured Card
   A secured card requires you to deposit money onto the
   card, which becomes the credit line.
Credit Card
   A payment card issued to users as a system of payment. It
   allows the cardholder to pay for goods and services based
   on the holder's promise to pay the money back with interest.
   You do not have to pay all the money back at the end of the
   month. You are only required to pay a minimum payment
   that the credit card company establishes toward the bill
   each month.

Let's look at some key terms associated with a credit card your child
should be aware of:

Annual Fee
   Yearly fee for having the card.
Annual Percentage Rate (APR)
   Allows you to evaluate the cost of the loan in terms of an
   annual percentage.
Annual Percentage Yield (APY)
   Similar to APR, however it is credited based off of com-
   pound interest. Creditors get more money from you by using
   this type of method.

Credit Line
  The amount you should not go over.
Cash Back/Rewards
  Incentives to having the card.
Balance
  What you owe.
Minimum Payment
  The lowest amount you can pay on your card.

Parents should help their child pick out a credit card if they want them to start building their credit correctly. When it comes to helping your child pick out a credit card, you should look for cards with the best features. You may use sites such as Bankrate.com, Credit.com, or Creditcards.com to help get you started. Make sure you reiterate the purpose for the card. Teach them ways to help them avoid falling into debt. You should also go over identity theft and how it should be handled at this time.

21ˢᵀ *Century Rich Kid Retirement Formula*

Before children leave home, it is important that parents talk about retirement and help them understand the necessary components in order for them to retire comfortably. Most children grow up believing they have to be sixty-five years old before they can retire. This is not true. Many parents miss the opportunity to help their children understand how they can retire early. Introducing your child to the 21ˢᵗ Century Rich Kid Formula will help your child have a better chance of retiring at their desired age.

Let's look at the key ingredients to consider in order for this to happen:

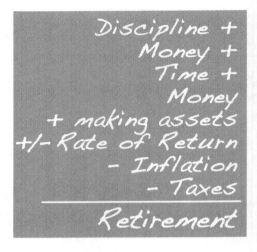

The first step to having a successful retirement is to have self-discipline. When you make the decision to be disciplined, you become laser-focused on completing the task at hand. The more disciplined you become, the more you increase your chances of having financial success. When a child develops a disciplined mindset early, it speeds up their journey to financial freedom. The fate of your retirement destiny depends on your consistency in following through and executing your strategy.

The second thing the formula states you need is money. At this age, your child should have some type of income, whether it is money they saved up, money from employment, or money from the products or services they offer as an entrepreneur. Parents should encourage their children to put away as much money as possible and utilize the concept of "living within your means" and cutting back on spending money on unnecessary purchases. The age of your child and the amount of money your child needs to retire will be the deciding factor of how much they save.

The third component is time. The younger your child starts saving money, the higher their chances of being able to retire sooner. Most people fail to retire at their desired age because of procrastination. This is the time to help your child get started if you want them to be able to live the best life possible.

The fourth component is investing in money-making assets. Having these types of assets will give you an opportunity to bring in more income. Assets give you a chance to earn passive income. This type of income keeps coming after you have done something only one time. For an example, if your child purchased some real estate and had tenants to pay rent to them every month, they would be receiving passive income. We will talk more about this type of income later in the book.

Self-Security is the New Retirement plan!

The next factor is the rate of return they receive on their money. This is the amount of money you receive back from an investment. It is determined by the financial product you invest your money in. Investments are ways to plan for your financial future by taking your money and placing it in a product that will give your money the opportunity to grow through receiving interest. There are certain products, such as stocks, where you could possibly lose money, so it is a good idea for your child to have a high level of risk tolerance before investing their money in these type of products.

Lastly, the formula shows you how inflation and taxes have a negative effect on your money by subtracting from it. Inflation is the rise of prices on goods and services. If you look back at the gas prices back in the 1980s compared to today, you will see how inflation has impacted the economy. The prices of things continue to rise, but the sad part is that most people's paychecks are not growing at the same rate. In order to beat taxes and inflation, you have to put your money in products that are giving you at least 5 percent interest or more. Within this book, you will learn how to capitalize on this amount of interest.

Helping your child understand this formula now will allow them to retire faster. This formula also gives your child a reason to want to put money away (pay yourself first) because they see they are in control of their future. This is also a good time to go over other key words related to the financial world with them. Let's look at some other definitions your children should be aware of when it comes to retirement/saving:

Wealth
    The abundance of assets and money that allows you to live a comfortable lifestyle.
Assets
    Anything you own that will be beneficial to you in the future.
Cash Flow
    The amount of money you have coming in and out on a continuous basis.
Asset Accumulation
    Using assets to help build wealth.
Real Estate
    Receiving money by selling property or renting out property you own.
S&P 500

The Standard and Poor's 500 is a financial index that fluctuates based on the performance of the top 500 companies in the United States. There are others, but this is the most popular one.

Dow Jones

This index represents thirty of the largest publicly owned and influential companies in the United States.

NASDAQ

This index stands for the National Association of Securities Dealers Automated Quotations. It is the second largest exchange in the United States and the world. This index includes some companies that are not based in the US.

Liabilities

Things that you purchase that don't bring about a profit in the future.

Net Worth

The amount you are worth based on your assets minus your liabilities.

Financial Portfolio

The different types of products you want to invest your money in.

Risk Management

Investing your money in a variety of products to lessen your chances of losing all of it.

As you enter the chapter on money-making assets, you will learn what types of products are available for your child to invest in for retirement. It is important that parents help their children put together a balanced portfolio to help them plan for their future. The age they want to retire at will play a major role when deciding what your children would like to invest their money in. Since most kids open up checking accounts to deposit their money in, it is necessary to teach them how to balance a checkbook before they leave home as well. As you begin to wrap up the Financial Head Start Program, you should revisit your child's financial roadmap and make sure you have gone through all the topics you wanted to cover. If there are areas you feel you want to work on a little more with your child, this is the time to go back over them. You want to make sure that by the time your child leaves home, they have the basic knowledge to help them make the right choices with their money. Once you have completed the checklist, it is a good idea to explain to your child what you did and encourage them to do the same thing with their children.

As children are introduced to these concepts during the transition stage, parents are equipping them to make the right financial choices beyond their childhood. As children transition to adulthood, they should be able to reflect on everything they learned through each stage of their financial development thus far. Preparing children before they leave home about the financial world gives them a higher chance of being able to live the lifestyle they desire.

The Coaching Phase

This phase covers ages eighteen years and beyond. Even though you may feel you are done raising your children after they leave home, you should still remain a financial parent. When your children have a question about how they should handle circumstances that may arise in their financial life, they should be able to pick up the phone and call you. You should be excited to help them. Even if you don't have all the answers, you can refer your children to someone who may be able to help them.

Being a financial parent is not about being an expert in the financial field. It is about helping expose your child to financial information that will help them understand the financial world better once they leave home. The more information you are able to give your child up front will help them make better decisions later. When you help your children become better with understanding money and building wealth, you are helping yourself as well.

The Financial Head Start Program was designed to keep things simple and help give children a general understanding about financial terminology before they become adults. Keep in mind, that the topics in this chapter were designed to give you an example of things to do with your child that will help put them on the right financial path. You may pick and choose the things you feel may be the most appropriate for your child based on their learning capabilities. If you feel your child is more advanced, you may choose to add more topics to discuss with them.

Planning Phase
Foundation Phase
Independent Phase
Transitioning Phase
Coaching Phase

By following the Financial Head Start Program, your children will be way ahead of kids their age whose parents are not financial parents. Your child doesn't have to wait until they go out and make financial mistakes to see that financial education is important. Principles taught in the program will help your child develop the right habits about money from the start. Your child will have a chance to enjoy their financial life by you teaching them prevention techniques up front.

Wealth Building

You must gain control over your money or the lack of it
will forever control you. - Dave Ramsey

4 Financial Accounts Children Should Have

Have you ever wondered how wealthy you could be if your parents had actually planned your financial future? If you are like me, you would jump for joy if that had happened. Unfortunately, as you have already learned, this is not the norm for most households. Most parents are not taking the necessary steps to help lead their children to financial success. Aside from not teaching financial skills, many parents are not setting money aside to invest in their children's financial future. Because of the lack of proper planning, children are left to make a life for themselves the best way they know how.

For some people, it is okay in their eyes for parents not to invest in their kid's financial future. However, when it comes to helping people have a better quality of life this is not okay. The truth is that for most households, wealth is not being passed down from generation to generation, but the cycle of living in debt is. It is my theory that if parents start teaching their children the proper financial education early while saving money with their children to help build for their future, more people would have a chance to experience a better way of living.

#openaccountsearly

We discussed earlier how using a financial roadmap can help parents ensure they are helping their children have the best financial life. By creating the plan, you will have a clearer view of which direction your child is headed financially. In the last chapter, we went through the different financial skills you should be covering on your roadmap. Now we are ready to talk about the financial accounts section of the roadmap. This is where you list the different financial accounts/products you would like to establish for your child.

It is important to define what types of accounts will work best for your child. There should be funds set aside for emergencies, planning for college, purchasing a new car, and buying daily necessities, as well as any other needs. Creating the financial roadmap helps you determine what products will be used to help your child reach their financial goals. Remember: As parents, you influence the financial direction that your children will take.

Why not build your child a better future than your parents did for you? There are different financial products that exist today to help guide you through the process. Let's look at some of the different

FUN ACCOUNTS	EMERGENCY ACCOUNTS	SCHEDULED ACCOUNTS
Prepaid Debit Cards	Savings Account	CDs
Savings/Checking	CDs	Money Markets
		529 College Savings Plan
		IRAs
		Stocks/Bonds
		Cash-Value Life Insurance

#openaccountsearly

types of accounts you can use to help build your children's financial portfolio.

Fun Accounts

The fun account has many uses. Before children are born, this type of account can be used to help parents start saving money that they will use specifically for their children's needs. Things such as diapers, wipes, and other necessities can be purchased with this account. This account allows parents to budget their money more effectively and to distinguish between money for their children and money out of their own personal account. This account helps make it easier for parents to keep track of how much they are spending on their children and allows them to continue to work on their own financial stability.

As you begin to introduce your children to financial institutions, opening a fun account for your children's personal use is beneficial. Your child will be able to get into the habit of saving money in a safe place away from home. Transferring money from the piggybank/savings jar is a great way to help fund the account. The account should be used to allow your child to make purchases they want.

Saving is important, but you have to allow your child the opportunity to purchase items they want as well. There should be a healthy balance between how much your child spends and how much they save. The fun account helps your child see the fun side of saving. Remember: It is important to keep your child excited about the savings process.

Opening up a savings or checking account at a bank or credit union for your child to save in is a great way to set up a fun account.

#openaccountsearly

Because your children will have access to their funds quickly with these types of accounts, they are more likely to be excited to get into the habit of saving. Your child is also able to receive a debit card with the accounts, which allows them to not have to carry around cash. This is a great feature because it helps ensure your children's safety.

These are ideal because they give your children a way to track their spending through a monthly statement. This helps you monitor if your child is abusing the account. Even though children use this account to make purchases, parents should make it a rule that a certain percentage of the money should not leave the account. This will help children form the habit of not spending all of their money just because they have it. Another way to establish a fun account is with a prepaid card. By using a prepaid card, parents are able to be in complete control over how much their children spend. The card has zero funds on it until you load it. It allows you to give your child a set amount of funds to make sure they purchase exactly what they are supposed to. It is easier than a regular debit card tied to an account because once they spend the money, they won't be able to have access to extra funds. It is best to purchase a reloadable prepaid card to get the most use from it.

Prepaid cards are appealing because they are designed to look like debit and credit cards. They allow you to make a purchase online, by phone, or in person. Impulse buying can be cut down by using these cards or just handing your child a set amount of cash they can spend. The biggest advantage about a prepaid card is that you, as the parent, control the card. The money your child saves in their savings account, checking account, savings jar, or piggybank should be used to fund the card.

#openaccountsearly

Emergency Accounts

Most people are not prepared for sudden events that may happen. According to an article written by Jeff Ellis in 2012 for CNN, 28 percent of Americans have no emergency savings.[5] It is important to help your child understand they need to begin saving for unexpected events that they may have no control over. When starting an emergency fund, two products you might consider are a savings account or a short-term savings vehicle such as a two year or less certificate of deposit (CD).

An emergency account is an account you can take money out of when unexpected expenses arise. It is important that you save your money in financial products where you can have quick access to your funds. The most common type of emergency account is a savings account. The reason being is that most people like to have easy access to their money without being penalized.

They don't want to have to pay extra fees to take their money out of products that carry a long-term agreement. There are different types of savings accounts. Some accounts are just basic savings accounts while others are accounts that give you a chance to receive compounding interest such as a money-market savings account and a high-yield savings account. These types of accounts come with several restrictions, so it is wise to sit down with a financial professional first and ask questions to see what the requirements are.

Most of the time with a money-market savings account and a high-yield savings account, you are granted a certain number of with-

---

[5] http://money.cnn.com/2012/06/25/pf/emergency-savings/

drawals every month and you have a higher amount that you have to deposit and maintain in the account. High-yield savings accounts are usually established online. The financial institution is able to give you a higher interest rate than normal because it is an online account. Many people find online banking to be more convenient.

I suggest you do your research about the accounts at financial institutions before you open an account because they all have their own rules. Although you don't get a lot of interest in a regular savings account, they are the most common because they are easier to set up. They are also appealing because of the low deposit associated with them. Most financial institutions only require a $25 deposit. However, beware of accounts that may charge you a certain fee if you don't maintain a certain balance.

If you decide you would like to start a CD for your child, you want to be sure it is a two years or less CD, so you will be able to see some type of savings, but you will not be caught up in a long-term contract. A shorter CD term will help lower the risk penalty when you are ready to withdraw the money. Hopefully, you won't need the money before the two years is up. If you are going to invest in a CD as an emergency fund, it is smart to put a little money aside in a regular savings account in case something happens before your money has reached maturity. We will talk more about CDs in the next section.

By setting up an emergency account for your child, you will be able to sign the account over to them when they turn eighteen. Making them help contribute to the account is the ultimate goal, even if you put money in there every once in a while. Not only will your child be amazed with how much easier life can be, but they will be encouraged to do the same thing for their children.

#openaccountsearly

Scheduled Accounts

Every child should have a scheduled account to help with college, big events, a new car, and other major things. Some ways to save are through certificates of deposits, money-market accounts, 529 plans, Individual Retirement Accounts (IRAs), and cash-value life insurance. By starting these types of accounts at birth, you have a chance to accumulate the most cash.

The most popular long-term scheduled account for most parents is saving for college. It is important to start saving for college to help cut down on the costs your children may incur later. When it comes to what types of financial products to use, the most popular products are 529 plans, Coverdell accounts, IRAs, stocks, bonds, and cash value life insurance. Let's look at how the 529 plan works.

The plan came out in 1996 and is now available in most states. Your state gets to decide if they want to carry one. It is an education plan that is operated by the state or an educational institution that helps give you an early start to saving money specifically for your child's college education. The name of the plan comes from Section 529 of the Internal Revenue Code.

It is important to check the requirements with the state you want to open up a plan in because each state has the choice of designing their own plan. A good thing about the plan is if one child decides they don't want to attend college, you can switch the plan over to another child who will attend college. The plan is appealing to many parents because it allows you special state and federal tax benefits if you meet a few basic requirements. You should keep in mind that this plan is only used for college, so if you take the money out for anything else you will be penalized.

You will also receive a 1099 form to complete and return to the IRS once you take the money out. When applying for financial aid, the 529 plan can affect your child's chances of receiving more money because the funds parents contributed to the education plan are to be listed under parental assets. Parental assets are usually factored as a maximum of 5.64 percent in determining the Expected Family Contribution.[6] Explore the pros and cons of the 529 plan in your state before you just jump in one.

Another way to begin saving for college is with a Coverdell Education Savings Account formerly known as the Education IRA. This account is a trust or custodial account that was created for the purpose of paying for qualified education expenses of the designated beneficiary. In addition to saving for college, these accounts can be used to fund educational expenses for kindergarten – high school. Parents can contribute to the account until the child reaches 18 *(unless the child is a special needs beneficiary).*

The account allows parents to put in a yearly contribution up to $2,000. If you contribute more, you will pay taxes. Your child will need to use the money in this account by the time they turn 30. These accounts can be set up at a bank, a mutual fund company, or a brokerage. Like a 529 plan, you can be penalized for taking money out for reasons other than cost toward college. If you know for sure your child is going to college, you may be interested in investing in a pre-paid tuition plan. You will need to check with your state to see if they are offered.

[6] http://www.savingforcollege.com/intro_to_529s/does-a-529-plan-affect-financial-aid.php

#openaccountsearly

Parents can also use their own IRAs to help pay for qualified higher education expenses. When used for college expenses, you are able to avoid the 10 percent penalty for the early withdrawal of funds. The Uniform Gifts to Minors Act (UGMA) and the Uniform Transfers to Minors Act (UTMA) are also custodial accounts used to save for college. These accounts allow parents to purchase securities for kids. Although you purchase the account, these types of accounts are turned over to your child from ages 18 to 21 depending on your state. Once children get an account, they can use it for whatever they want to.

Parents who have a high risk tolerance use stocks to save. Many professionals suggest that you start out saving with stocks while your child is young and switch to bonds as they get older.

When it comes to bonds, make sure you choose ones that will benefit you and your child the most. Because bonds are no longer sold at banks, savings-and-loans, and credit unions, the number of people who purchase them have decreased. You are still able to purchase bonds online on sites such as TreasuryDirect.com or complete paper bonds at tax time. Although there are several types of bonds you may choose to invest in, many people still use the EE savings bond to help their kids save for college.

With this type of bond, the government tells you the interest rates for the bonds on May 1 and November 1 of every year. Interest rates for these bonds have gone down over the years, causing many parents not to find them appealing anymore. For new bonds that were opened between May 1, 2014, and October 31, 2014, the interest rates were only 0.50 percent.[7] The low interest has turned many

[7] http://www.treasurydirect.gov/indiv/research/indepth/ebonds/res_e_bonds.htm

people away from the product, but if you are looking to start a savings vehicle for your child for as low as $25, this may be an option for you.

The key is to have a balanced portfolio. Because most people don't like to put their eggs in one basket, they purchase mutual funds to create diversification and invest in lower risk products. When deciding what types of investments you are comfortable with, it is important to assess the risk. Keep in mind, putting stocks in your child's name can cause your child to receive less money for financial aid.

If your risk tolerance is not very high, I would suggest you invest in life insurance with a cash value for your child's education. Life insurance policies with cash value allow you to withdraw loans against the cash value tax free. If you try to surrender the entire policy, you will be subject to paying income taxes. You want to keep your money in a policy for at least ten to fifteen years to actually see growth in your cash value before you make a withdrawal.

Unlike 529 plans and Coverdell accounts, you are not penalized for using the money in the cash-value life insurance for something else if your child does not attend college. Loans and withdrawals from life insurance policies can be used for any kind of expenses. Most people only think of life insurance when someone passes away, but there are several benefits to life insurance when you purchase the right product. If you are more comfortable with putting your money in an account with fixed interest, life insurance can give you an opportunity to gain higher interest. We will talk more about this later.

Not only is it important to save for your children's education, but it

[7] http://www.treasurydirect.gov/indiv/research/indepth/ebonds/res_e_bonds.htm

#openaccountsearly

is also important to help your child start long-term savings where they can begin building wealth for themselves. We talked about having a CD for an emergency account, but it can also be used as a long-term investment. The longer you keep your money in a CD, the greater your chance is to gain more interest. The most common types of certificate of deposits, or CDs are traditional, liquid, brokerage, and bump ups.

Traditional CDs are the most popular because they give you a fixed interest rate. Once the term you committed to expires, you can either take your money from the bank or you can roll it over into another CD. During that period, you are able to increase the amount of money you put into the account at most financial institutions. If you would like to continue contributing money to your account after you open it, then you should consider add-on CDs. There are penalties associated with both types of CDs when you decide to withdraw the funds before the maturity date.

Liquid CDs allow you to take money out after a set period of time before the maturity date. You are normally required to keep a certain minimum balance to avoid any penalties. There are limits on when you can withdraw the money. The interest rate is normally lower than a traditional CD since it is more flexible.

Brokerage CDs are handled by brokers. These certificates normally have higher rates than a traditional CD. They can be traded like bonds; however, you risk the chance of losing money. Just like bank products, this certificate is protected by the Federal Deposit Insurance Corporation (FDIC) as long as you keep the money in until the maturity date and the broker places your money with a FDIC bank. Make sure you know your risks before you invest in this type of product.

#openaccountsearly

Bump-up certificates have become popular because they allow you to switch to a higher interest rate per term. If you discover that the bank has increased the interest rate after you have had the certificate a few months, you can call and ask them to move your money to a higher interest. Keep in mind you can only do this once per term, so choose wisely when you ask the bank to bump up your rate until the maturity date. If you are looking to change the interest rate multiple times, you may be interested in a step-up CD.

When you are looking to open any type of certificate of deposit, there are a few things you need to know. First, how much do you need to invest and how much interest are you going to receive. We will talk more about interest in the next chapter. Most banks express the interest you can earn in a CD as the Annual Percentage Yield (APY). Because there are different types of CD products, you need to make sure you understand all the terms and conditions. Beware of products like variable-rate CDs, step-down CDs, or bump-up CDs where the interest rate can change or any additional fees can be added.

Another important thing you want to find out is when the CD will mature and how much you will be penalized for early withdrawal. Don't get so caught up with the interest rate that you forget to get any information about any penalties involved if you withdraw the funds before the maturity date. It might not be a wise idea to put your money in a certain type of CD if it doesn't give you an opportunity to take out a certain amount without paying any fees. Keep in mind that every institution is different.

Because CDs are covered by the FDIC, they are very appealing. They are also great to invest in because they allow you to have a long- or short-term savings option. As we discussed earlier, the dis-

#openaccountsearly

advantage of a CD is the penalties you could face for withdrawing your money early. Another disadvantage to having a CD is paying taxes on it every year.

If you decide not to use a money-market account as an emergency account, you may want to use it as an scheduled account. Most people are not aware that a money-market account is a savings and an investment account. The two types of money-market accounts are deposit accounts and mutual funds. As I stated before, money-market accounts require you to maintain a certain balance. They are similar to regular saving accounts because they allow you to have check-writing and money-transferring privileges.

Your funds are usually invested in short-term, fixed securities like US Treasuries. These types of accounts require you to put in a larger amount of money. By putting a larger sum of money in the account, you have a chance to get the best interest rate. There are no penalties for taking your money out early. Remember you are limited in the number of withdrawals you are able to take out.

Most customers who purchase money-market accounts use them until they find a better place to put their money. Over the long term, money-market accounts don't keep up with inflation, causing them to be less appealing than other products. There are a few differences between the two types of money-market accounts that you need to keep in mind. Deposit accounts are protected by the FDIC, whereas mutual funds are not. You have a chance to receive higher interest in a mutual fund, but you could also lose money as well.

Stocks, bonds, mutual funds and cash-value life insurance are not only good for college-funding, but they are also products that should be considered for building long-term wealth. Your child will need money for things in life other than college-funding. For example, you can take money from any of these accounts and help your child purchase their first car, help finance a business, help pay for a wedding, and the list goes on. The scheduled account should be purchased while your child is a baby. It is the most important account because it helps determine the number of years your children have to save towards building wealth. Because parents are in control of all the accounts we discussed, you can pick and choose what products are best for your child. If you want to use a 529 college savings plan or a Coverdell account as your college-funding vehicle, it is wise to open up one of the other accounts to help start building wealth.

In addition to establishing these accounts for their children, it is wise for parents to have legacy accounts such as a life insurance policy, a living trust, and a will in place for themselves, so that their children are still set up for financial success in the event something were to happen to them. A life insurance policy allows your children to receive money to continue moving forward comfortably by giving them what is known as a death benefit. A will is a legal document that allows you to assign your property over to whoever you choose. If your children are young, you are also able to make sure they will have the proper guardian to look after them. You risk the government taking over your estate and distributing it the way they would like by not having one.

Purchasing a living trust gives you an opportunity to store all of your assets in one place and still have control of them. Your trust includes things such as your home, your banking accounts, stocks, bonds, and mutual funds. You are able to benefit from these things while you are alive and pass them to your beneficiary when you die. It is

#openaccountsearly

important to have these three things in place if you want to make sure your children have the opportunity to have a better quality of life with or without you here. Parents are responsible for making sure their children are set up for the best financial future possible regardless of the circumstances.

It is important for parents to think every situation through when planning for their children's future. There should be products in place that have living benefits as well as death benefits. Meeting with a financial professional is a good idea when you are trying to put together a portfolio of products. Having a strategic plan and the necessary financial products prepared ahead of time to address the circumstances life may bring makes things a lot easier for you and your children.

5

The Power of Interest-Bearing Accounts

When you are establishing scheduled accounts to help build wealth for your child, it is important to consider accounts where you can gain the most interest. As you decide what accounts you want to set up, you should take the amount of interest you can receive and how the interest is credited into consideration. Financial products with interest as a feature can offer you simple interest or compound interest. Most people are not aware of the two types. Let's look at how interest works:

Simple vs. Compound Interest

Let's say you had a $1,000 to deposit and you wanted to save it at your local bank. As you are discussing your financial plans with your banker, they recommend a product that can offer you 5 percent simple interest per year. So that means after year one, you would have earned $50. The next year you would earn another $50, but it would be based on your $1,000 deposit even though you really had $1,050 in your account. You will not be able to receive interest based on the $1,050 because simple accounts don't allow you to earn interest on top of interest. You are only able to gain interest off your initial deposit.

Because you are only able to gain interest off the initial deposit, it will take longer for your money to grow. That is why I suggest that you open up accounts that allow your child to receive compounding interest. Compounding interest allows you to grow interest on top of interest, which gives you a chance to grow your money faster. If the account you open offered compounding interest, you would have been able to receive 5 percent on top of the $1,050. The second year, you would have $1102.50. The fifth year, you would have $1,276.28.

As you can see, compounding interest can help you grow your money much faster. Most people know how to earn money but never learn how to make their money work for them. The lack of knowledge has caused several people to misuse their funds. If you have not learned the Rule of 72 by now, you might be mismanaging your money. The mathematical formula, created by Albert Einstein, shows you the power of compounding interest by taking the number 72 and dividing it by your interest rate to see how long it will take for your money to double.

Rule of 72

72 ÷ Interest Rate

The approximate number
of years it takes to double
your money

#isyourmoneygrowing

Example:

Ashley, a twenty-five year old grad student is looking to invest 10,000 to start saving toward her retirement. Based on the table, which interest rate would give her the best rate of return and allow her to grow her money the fastest?

Disclaimer: This chart does not represent a specific product; it is only being used for illustrative purposes. It does not guarantee that these figures will be your actual return.

AGE	72 ÷2=36	AGE	72 ÷8=9	AGE	72 ÷12=6
MONEY DOUBLES EVERY 36 YEARS		**MONEY DOUBLES EVERY 9 YEARS**		**MONEY DOUBLES EVERY 6 YEARS**	
25	10,000	25	10,000	25	10,000
61	20,000	34	20,000	31	20,000
97	40,000	43	40,000	37	40,000
		52	80,000	43	80,000
		61	160,000	49	160,000
				55	320,000
				61	640,000
				67	1,280,000

If someone were to save $10,000 dollars at the age of twenty-five and they were to put their money in an account offering them 2 percent interest, then based on the Rule of 72, their money would double every thirty-six years. If they put the same amount of money in an account giving them 8 percent, the money would double every nine years. If they put money into an account giving them 12 percent interest, their money would double every six years. Based on the Rule of 72, it is best to get a higher interest rate when you are storing your money in financial accounts. Therefore, the answer to the question I just gave you would be 12 percent. The earlier the person begins saving will also play a role in how much time they have to actually see their money grow.

When choosing what types of financial accounts you want to open, you should be sure you are getting the highest interest possible. Most people don't understand the importance of using the Rule of 72 to build wealth faster. They normally open up bank accounts that give them less than 2 percent and wonder why they are not getting wealthy. It is important to research what products will help you reach your personal savings goals.

When setting financial goals, most people choose to only do business with a bank rather than diversify their money when it comes to their savings goals. They don't realize there are other financial products they can benefit from. They also don't realize how banks operate. Have you ever wondered how banks can loan you money and still manage? They take our money and invest it to make a bigger profit. Most people run to the bank for all their financial needs, but the truth is that you should diversify your money by placing it in different types of investments. Placing all of your eggs in one basket will lead you to financial failure.

If you look around, you will find that most big banks are paying less than 1 percent in traditional savings accounts. Some banks are paying up to 2.35 percent in five-year CDs. That is an improvement from previous years. When checking interest rates on different products, it is a good idea to shop around with different companies to make sure you are receiving the best rates.

The average person doesn't get rich just by working hard, but rather they become rich by allowing their money to work for them by using compound interest. If you were to invest $600 a month getting 8 percent interest for 30 years, you would have $894, 215. For many people, this amount of money is more than enough to enjoy retirement. However, most people don't get a chance to save a lot of money because they are too busy buying things that they don't really need.

As a result, they struggle to get where they want to be. To help your children get into a good savings habit, it is important to help them understand the importance of cutting back on their expenses. In order to save at least $200 a month, teach your children how to cut back on things such as eating out, partying, and buying bottled water. The earlier your children become consistent with saving their money and using products with compounding interest, the higher the chance that they will be able to live their desired lifestyle.

Many people are unaware that there are products around giving you 8 percent and up without you having to lose money. So why is it that not everyone is investing in these types of products? Why is it that some people retire faster than others? Why is it harder for some people to become financially independent?

I believe there are three reasons people struggle financially. We have already discussed the first reason: they are "instant people" who want everything now and never plan ahead and save their money. They procrastinate year after year, and the older they get, the more expensive saving gets.

The second reason is because people just don't know what is out here to help them live a better life. The lack of financial education has caused people to make bad spending decisions and never start saving. And the third reason people struggle financially is because people are living longer. The life expectancy has increased over the years. For some who didn't plan properly that means they may have to go back to work.

It is my hope that after reading this book, you and your family will not fall into either category. Most people say knowledge is power, but the truth is if you don't use your knowledge, it is not powerful at all. We spend so much time planning weddings, birthday parties, and different events, but how much time do we actually spend on our financial future?

In the same way the Rule of 72 works for you, it can also work against you. Say you have a credit card and the interest rate is 24 percent. It only takes three years for your debt to double. Most people never see the positive side from the Rule of 72 because they are trapped in debt. That is why you need to be cautious when you begin applying for credit cards and other loans. Credit cards and other loan providers allow you to only pay a minimum balance each month because they benefit from you not paying more up front because you end up paying them more money back.

For example: If you had a credit card with a $3,000 balance with an interest rate of 22 percent and only paid the minimum payment of $120 a month, it would take you 34 months to pay off. The total interest would be $1,050. That means you would be paying back a total of $4,050 for your initial loan amount.

Let's say you decided to pay $50 extra a month. If you paid $170 a month it would take twenty-two months. The total interest paid will be $658. You would pay back a total of $3,658.

As you can see, paying $120 versus $170 a month makes a major difference. Paying more than your minimum payment definitely saves you some money in the long run. Companies giving you higher interest rates benefit from the minimum payment because you are only paying back the interest in the early years before you even start paying off the principal amount. The minimum payment is designed to help companies earn as much interest as possible from you.

When it comes to refinancing accounts such as a money loan or car loan, you should be very cautious. Most of the time when you refinance, you are starting over. That's why you should not just sign up for things without knowing what is required of you. Instead of just looking at the money you are receiving up front, it is a good idea to focus on a smart game plan to pay off loans and credit cards as quickly as possible.

I remember when I got my first job at the age of sixteen. I was excited that I was making my own money and doing things I wanted to do. I remember getting my check every two weeks and paying my first car note and insurance. After I took care of my bills, I was free to do whatever I wanted with my money. I had an account, but I did not have any idea how to invest. If I would have started paying myself first, I would have been far more ahead than I was after I graduated college.

As parents, we can't relive our childhood, but we can start rebuilding our households by incorporating financial living skills. I blew my money as a teenager, but instead of dwelling on it now, I choose to go out and empower other young people by teaching them the power of compounding interest. Who would have thought something as simple as the Rule of 72 could have so much effect on your financial life? Now let's look at places where you have the opportunity to gain interest.

Places that offer products with compounding interest

The three places most people invest their money are the bank, investments, and insurance. People like the bank because their money is insured by the FDIC, but they dislike the low interest rates. Banks also allow people to have quick access to their money. Some people like the idea of keeping all of their money in one place.

Investment accounts are appealing because they allow you to gain a lot of interest, but the downfall is you can lose money. In the 2008 financial crisis, there was a downturn in stock markets around the world. Stocks and bonds can take you on a roller coaster ride. Most people who invest in these products have a high risk tolerance. If you don't have a high risk tolerance, you should consider other places to invest.

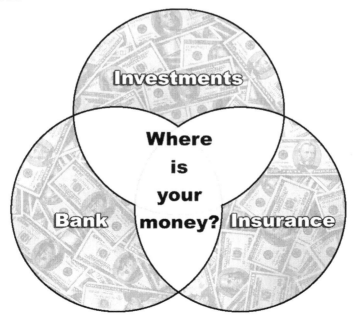

#isyourmoneygrowing

Cash-value life insurance is a place people store money because you have the opportunity to get some of the same benefits as a bank and an investment. People like the fact that their money is safe, and they don't have to risk losing it in the stock market. They also like the fact that they have an opportunity to get more interest in their account than they would receive from a bank. Unlike the other two places, you have an opportunity to leave a tax-free death benefit to your beneficiary if something were to happen to you.

All three places have helped people gain financial success. You have to decide whether you want to move slow or fast. Do you want to have an opportunity to gain the most interest? Are you more concerned with safety and never losing money? Do you want to save on taxes? These are all questions you need to ask yourself.

When it comes to helping your child build wealth, financial products with compounding interest ensure that you will have the best chance to do so. Using an account earning compound interest helps your money grow faster. Although there are many great benefits with this type of interest, we have to keep in mind that it can work against us when applying for credit cards and other loans. As parents, we have to make sure our children understand the positive side and negative side to interest in order to help them save as much money as possible.

6

The 21ST Century Savings Tool

Have you ever wondered where you could invest your money, get a decent interest rate, never lose money, and refrain from paying taxes all at the same time? That would be a great product don't you think? What if I told you that product does exist, and it is the 21ST Century Savings Tool? Ok, so maybe now I have your attention if you thought there was no such product.

When it comes to saving, it is important to figure out what products meet your financial goals. If you haven't shopped around for different products, you are probably one of the thousands of people who have missed out on an opportunity to save more money. In the last two chapters, we briefly discussed different products that your child could benefit from. In this chapter, we will discuss how the 21st Century Savings Tool is helping people reach financial freedom.

So by now you are probably wondering what product I am talking about. The product has been around for years, but a lack of financial education has kept people from reaping the full benefits of it. This

#neverlosemoney

product has been updated several times to help give consumers a better way to save. If you haven't guessed what I am talking about by now, the secret product is cash-value life insurance. To be more exact, I am referring to index life insurance products.

Who would have thought life insurance products could lead to financial success while you are still alive. Life insurance became popular when Congress exempted it from income taxes in 1913. Since then, several products have been created. Although the products carry different features, they all benefit you by providing a tax-free death benefit to your beneficiaries.

With the turn of the 21st century, life insurance has been transformed to be more than just a protection plan. After the market went down in the early 2000s, Americans were in need of a breakthrough in the financial sector. The days of just purchasing life insurance in case someone passed away have faded. With the inception of index products, life insurance can be a savings tool for anything you want. Most people have never heard of index products because traditional insurance companies still use outdated products. Index products are products where you have a chance to receive interest in your account based on the performance of different indices such as the S&P 500. The S&P 500 is the most common index used. It is composed of the top 500 companies in the US and their market capitalizations. By investing in index products, you have the opportunity to gain higher interest.

Some people believe in the concept of *"buy term, invest the rest."* Depending on what you invest in, you could risk losing money. Index products allow you a chance to capitalize on a decent amount of interest without the risk of losing any money.

#neverlosemoney

Temporary life insurance consists of term insurance. These products are similar to renting an apartment. When you have an apartment, you sign a lease for a certain amount of time before you have to renew the contract again. The same is true for term products. You can purchase a policy for five, ten, fifteen, twenty, twenty-five, thirty, or thirty-five years. If you do not pass away during the specific time period, your policy will expire.

Term = Temporary

Term products are inexpensive in the beginning, but they become more expensive the older you are. When renewing a policy, you may have to pay a new amount based on your current age. Depending on what type of policy you have, you may have to retake your medical exam. It is also important to keep in mind that your health changes daily, which could cause you not to qualify for a policy.

Because companies are different and carry different products, it is a good idea to schedule an appointment with a financial professional to get all of your questions answered. There have been several instances where people thought they had a permanent policy, but it was really a temporary policy. The truth is that some agents focus more on their commission checks than on properly educating their clients. Don't allow your family to suffer because you thought you had a permanent policy when you really had a term policy that has already expired.

If you are not struggling with your finances, I would suggest you look into purchasing a permanent product. There are some companies that will allow you to upgrade to a permanent policy after having a term policy for a set amount of time. No matter what your situation is, you should have some type of policy in place. Let's look at the benefits of having a permanent policy.

There are four types of permanent policies: whole life, universal life, variable life, and index universal life. Each one of them allows you to gain interest on your money in the cash value, also known as your savings account. A portion of the premium you pay goes toward policy charges and the rest goes into the cash value. Most companies allow you to overfund the cash value to a certain extent. Each policy has its own unique features.

Whole life insurance was the first permanent product to enter the marketplace. The product allows you to have a fixed premium and a fixed death benefit. These policies are usually the most expensive.

You can usually gain up to 2–4 percent interest in the cash value. The money saved in the cash value can only be used while the policyholder is living. If something happens to the individual, the beneficiary will only get the fixed death benefit amount, not the money in the cash value.

Example: Let's say you have a death benefit amount of $500,000, and you have a set premium of $150. Before you passed away, you had $3,000 saved in your cash value. Because there is a fixed death benefit, your beneficiary will not receive the money in the cash value. Your beneficiary will only get the $500,000. These products are typically not flexible.

In the 1980s, universal life insurance became popular. This type of policy allows clients to have a flexible premium and flexible death benefit. If you get behind on your payments, you are able to use the money in your cash value to help pay your premium. You have the potential to gain between 3–5 percent interest rate in your cash value.

Example: You have a death benefit amount of $500,000, and your premium is $150. If you get ill for a couple of months and have money in your cash value, you are able to use the funds until you are able to start paying the premium again. If you have $3,000 in your cash value and you pass, your beneficiary can get up to $503,000, depending on how your policy is set up.

In the 1990s, variable life became popular. A portion of your money goes toward the cost of insurance and the other portion goes into a separate account such as a mutual fund. The interest in the cash value is credited based on how well the stock market is doing. When purchasing this type of product, you have to assess your risk tolerance. You have a chance to get a higher interest rate, but there is also a chance you could lose money. This product was very appealing until the market went down drastically in the early 2000s.

Important note: The only difference between a variable universal life and a regular universal life is that you have a chance of losing more money in your cash value because you are investing in accounts similar to mutual funds where the interest rates can fluctuate. You can incur a negative interest rate as a result, causing you to lose the majority of your savings. If your risk tolerance is low, you might want to consider another product.

After the market crashed, variable life products became less popular. People were devastated about the money they had lost. Those

#neverlosemoney

who had invested in the stock market realized that it was much more risky than they had expected. Due to losing so much money, many people began to search for new ways to save. As a result, index life insurance products began to rise in popularity.

These products have given people the opportunity to get a decent interest rate without incurring any risk. Index products have allowed people to incorporate the concept of never losing money. This powerful concept has allowed people to save more money. These products are appealing because they allow consumers to receive interest rates by working indirectly with the stock market.

As you saw earlier in the chapter, insurance companies use different indices, such as the S&P 500, to credit you your interest rate. Some insurance companies also use international indices, such as the Euro Stoxx 50 and Hang Seng. Because your interest rate is credited by working with the stock market indirectly, companies give you a set interest rate that you can gain, known as the cap, and a guaranteed interest rate you will never go under, known as the floor. The set amounts differ for each company, but they all guarantee you will not lose money.

For instance, some companies will give you up to 15 percent interest with a guarantee of at least .75 percent.

That means that if the S&P 500 index went up 20 percent, the company would credit you 15 percent because that is their cap, but it also means that if that same index went down by 12 percent, you would get a guaranteed .75 interest rate because that is their floor. If the percentage was 8 percent, you would get 8 percent because it falls in between the cap and the floor amounts. Your money would

#neverlosemoney

always be growing. Different companies offer different percentages, but the overall objective is to help people never lose money.

These products carry several characteristics. They are similar to banking products because they are safe. Life insurance customers are protected by their state's department of insurance. They are like investments because they give you a chance to see your money grow. The fact that it is an insurance policy allows you to reap the tax benefits and still have protection if something happens to you. This product is a must-have in your financial portfolio.

When shopping for these products, their official names are Index Universal Life Insurance (IUL) and Global Index Universal Life Insurance (GIUL). One obvious difference is that one credits your interest rate based on the American market, and the other gives you an opportunity to utilize global markets. Because they are universal life products, they carry the same benefits of traditional universal life insurance. Let's look at how you might benefit from a GIUL product. Some global index products allow you to receive a higher interest rate than you would receive just using the American market. For an example, say your GIUL interest rate was based on the S&P 500, the Euro Stoxx 50, and the Hang Seng indices. The company would credit you 50 percent of the top performing index, 30 percent of the second highest index, and 20 percent of the third highest index. They would add the numbers up and based on the amount they calculate, you would be credited toward your interest rate. Remember: There is a set cap you are not able to go over.

As you can see, life insurance has definitely transformed its image. In the past, many people have been more concerned with the price and the discounts they could receive when they added life insurance to an existing insurance policy. By focusing on these things, people have missed products that can help lead them to financial success faster. Many adults have begun to use index universal life products to help build a tax-free retirement.

As we have already discussed, many parents also purchase cash-value life insurance policies to help with college-funding. The rates for purchasing a permanent policy for a child are much cheaper than it is for an adult. These policies allow you to put extra money toward the cash value part in your policy up to a certain amount aside from your monthly payments. By allowing you to overfund, the policy you have a greater chance to gain interest on a greater

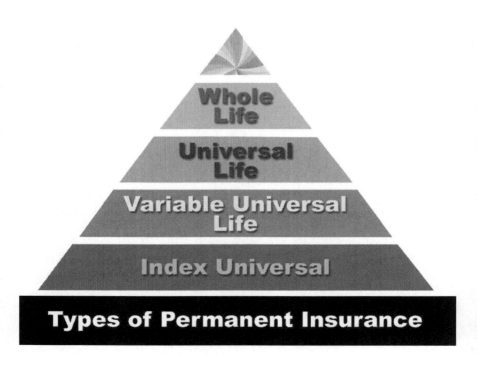

amount of money. This will allow you to accumulate wealth faster. Another benefit of having a permanent product is the tax advantages you can receive. Make sure you utilize the money correctly to capitalize on not paying taxes. Remember: Life insurance is a long-term investment. You should keep the money in the cash value for at least ten years or longer to avoid paying any type of fees associated with taking money early from the policy.

Top 10 Reasons to Purchase an IUL

1. It's a great way to participate in the market without the market risk.

2. You own the account even if it is for your child.

3. You have the potential to gain between 10–14 percent annually.

4. You have access to the money regardless of your age without an IRS penalty.

5. You can start your children's education fund.

6. You can start a retirement plan.

7. You are allowed to overfund the account.

8. You can take out loans and withdrawals when needed. *(I suggest after ten or fifteen years to avoid fees.)*

9. There is a tax-free death benefit.

10. It is a quality product that allows you:

Now you can stop wondering if there is a product that exists that can give you safety, a decent amount of growth, tax advantages, and protection all in one place. **The answer is clear**: Index Universal Life Insurance products are the best savings tool for the 21st century.

CHAPTER 7

The Effects of Taxes

I remember when I started my first job and had to complete my new-hire paperwork. I was clueless about how to fill out my tax forms. I really didn't understand how to make deductions and what it meant to be exempt from paying taxes. I asked another new hire sitting beside me how to fill the forms out and she didn't know how to either. When I got my first check, I didn't understand why I had so much money taken out of my check. I had so many questions and concerns. No one took the time to explain to me what the different taxes on my paycheck were. The only tax I was familiar with was the federal income tax. I knew that people got excited around the beginning of the year when they filed their income taxes. It felt like Christmas all over again as I watched people buy new cars, new furniture, new clothes, and make other purchases.

Taxes were a subject that I found hard to understand growing up. As I started talking with others, they told me they had stories similar to mine when they got their first jobs. Some parents make the mistake of assuming their kids will automatically learn about important subjects on their own. This should not be the case when it comes to taxes.

As a parent, you should discuss taxes with your children to help them understand why they are important. No one likes to pay them, but they are mandatory. Taxes are special fees paid by citizens that state and federal governments impose on products, activities, and income. The government uses taxes to help fund federal and state programs and projects. When you talk to your children about taxes, it is a good idea to discuss the different types that may be deducted from their paycheck.

You don't have to go through all the taxes and make things complicated, but discussing the most common taxes—such as those that appear on paychecks, sales taxes, and property taxes—is a good place to start. As we discussed earlier, going over their paycheck with them is a good way to help get the conversation started. By explaining to them what each tax pays for, they will be more informed about where their money is going.

The most familiar tax that people are used to paying is the federal income tax. Federal income taxes go toward a number of programs, such as national defense, foreign affairs, law enforcement, education, and transportation. When your child gets a job, they are able to complete tax forms where they decide how they want to be taxed and can select as many deductions as they qualify for. As you talk about federal income taxes, it is a good time to go over how to complete new-hire tax forms.

When teens and adults start working, they are likely to see the tax automatically deducted from their paychecks. If your teen is self-employed and makes over 6300^{2015}, they are required to report their income taxes to the government. Being self-employed has its benefits, because at the end of the year when it is time to file your

#legallystoppayingtaxes

income taxes, you may write off your expenses, which can help you lower your chances of having to pay a penalty. A penalty is when you owe the government.

Another tax deducted is the Social Security tax. The Social Security tax helps provide monthly benefits to retired and disabled workers, their dependents, and their survivors. The Medicare tax is also deducted. Medicare provides health insurance for Americans age sixty-five and older who have worked and paid into the system. It also provides health insurance to younger people with disabilities. These taxes are part of the Federal Insurance Contributions Act (FICA. Unlike income taxes, you don't have a choice not to pay FICA.

Most people have state taxes deducted from their paycheck if their state requires it. Some even have local taxes deducted. All the taxes we have discussed so far are the most common taxes deducted from your paycheck if you are a W2 employee.

Other important taxes that we are required to pay are sales taxes. They are taxes we incur when we make a purchase or go to an activity. For example, if I see some shoes for $9.99 and get to the cash register and the price is $10.32, the extra money is going toward the sales tax. Many local and state governments carry this tax to help fund projects such as paving new roads. Everyone has to pay sales taxes. There are not any exceptions because of your age.

Property taxes are another subject you should briefly discuss. Property taxes are paid on your home each year. If the tax charges are not paid within a certain period of time, you have the chance of losing your home if you own it. Each jurisdiction—whether it is the national government, a state, a county or geographical location, or a municipality—may control how property taxes will be handled. Be aware that multiple jurisdictions can tax the same property. It is a good idea to research the jurisdiction you live in to see what the guidelines are.

The reason I chose to discuss these taxes is because they are taxes that your children have a higher chance of paying when they get older. Because taxes can be complicated, it is smart to keep things simple at this point. Going over these basic taxes will help give your child a basic understanding of what different taxes are. If you are not comfortable talking about taxes with your child, another option is to reach out to a tax professional.

Financial Products That Can Save You from Paying Taxes

As we discussed earlier, it is important to help get your children's accounts started when they are young to help them create the most wealth. When making a decision about what products to use, you want to be cautious of what tax category the different products fall into to avoid paying more money in taxes than you will receive in interest. Financial products fall into three tax categories: tax annually, tax future, or tax maybe.

Tax annually products consist of mostly banking products. Every year you receive a 1099 to pay taxes on these accounts. Because you receive little interest on these products, you will often find yourself losing money because you pay more in taxes than you actually gain in interest each year.

TAX ANNUALLY	TAX FUTURE	TAX MAYBE
You pay taxes every year	You pay taxes when you withdraw	You don't have to pay taxes *(when the money is used correctly)*
Savings/Checking	401(k) / 403(b)	Roth IRAs
CDs	IRAs	Cash-Value Life Insurance
Money Market	Variable Annuities	529 College Savings Plans
Your paycheck	Fixed Annuities	Municipal Bond
Mutual Funds	Savings Bonds	
Stocks/Bonds		
Treasuries		

Let's say you deposited money into two different accounts. One that gives you 3 percent interest and one that gives you 5 percent interest.

> **Initial Investment**   **$200.00**
> **Fixed Interest 3 percent**   **+ $6.00**
> _____
> **$206.00**

When you are ready to withdraw your money let's say you have to pay 20 percent in federal taxes and 5 percent in state taxes.

> **$6.00 x .25 = $1.50**

So that means from your $206, you would pay $1.50 in taxes

> **$206.00 - 1.50 = $204.50**

Then you still have to pay inflation. Let's say the inflation level was 3.5 percent.

> **$200.00 x .035 = $7.00**

Real Rate of Return: $204.50 - $7.00 = $197.50

As you can see in this example, the effects of taxes and inflation have a great impact on how much your actual return will be when dealing with tax annually products. If you were to go back and plug in 5 percent interest, your actual return would come out to be $200.50. This example helps you see the importance of receiving an interest rate of 5 percent and higher in order to beat taxes and inflation. When opening products that fall into the tax annually category, be sure to factor in taxes and inflation to see what your actual return could be. Even though you may have to pay taxes, it is still smart to have products that are taxed annually in your financial portfolio to help diversify your money.

The next category is tax future products. Tax future accounts are mainly retirement accounts. These accounts don't tax you while you are contributing the funds, but when you are ready to start using the funds, you will be taxed. Most retirement accounts are a 401(k), 403(b), annuities, or IRAs.

A 401(k) is a retirement account that you may open with your employer if the program is available. Most employers will usually match the amount of money you contribute to help you build your retirement. 403(b) plans are similar to a 401(k), but they are mainly for public-school workers. Schools can set the plan up through custodial accounts that are invested in mutual funds like a 401(k), or they may open up an annuity contract from an insurance company.

When someone opens an annuity, they make an investment into the annuity, and in return, they are able to capitalize on receiving a steady cash flow when they are ready to begin withdrawing the funds at the designated retirement age.

When it comes to an IRA, these accounts are normally established by small business owners. The most common ones are the traditional IRA, Simplified Employee Pension IRA (SEP IRA), and the Savings Incentive Match Plan for Employees IRA (SIMPLE IRA). The differences between these types of accounts are their restrictions based on your income or employment status. They all have a cap on the amount of money you can contribute each year. All the products we discussed in this category will not only tax you when you take money out, but you will receive a 10 percent penalty if you take the money out before the designated retirement age.

Most bonds are also placed into this category. Bonds require you to pay federal income taxes on the interest when you are ready to cash it out. A few exceptions to that rule are when you use your Series EE or I Bond to pay for tuition at a qualified higher learning institution. When you do that, you are exempted from paying federal income taxes.

If you use the bond for anything else, you will be subject to paying taxes. When it comes to reporting your interest, you have a choice on how you report it. Some people choose to report their interest every year instead of waiting until the bond matures. Whether you are reporting interest at the end of the bond's life or every year, you report the interest from your bonds on your federal income tax return on the same line with other interest income.

The last tax category is tax maybe products. These products help prevent you from paying taxes if you go about using them the correct way. These products include 529 college savings plans, Roth IRAs, cash-value life insurance, and municipal bonds. Each product has restrictions you must follow to prevent you from having to pay taxes.

529 plans are not subject to federal tax or state taxes *(usually)* when the money is used for education expenses such as tuition, fees, books, or room and board. The contributions adults make to the plan are not deductible. As we discussed earlier, if the child you set the plan up for does not want to attend college, you may switch the plan over to another child. When this plan is not used for educa-

tional funding, you will have to pay taxes on the money.

Roth IRAs are different from the IRAs we previously discussed in the tax future section because they allow you to have tax breaks if they are used correctly. Roth IRAs are funded with after-tax dollars, meaning you already paid taxes on the money you put in. After you put the money in a Roth IRA, you won't be taxed again. This is very appealing because you get to keep all the earnings you made from your interest. As long as you don't plan to withdraw the money before the designated retirement age, you won't have to pay taxes again. Like the other retirement accounts, you will receive a 10 percent penalty and pay taxes if you take the money out before you are fifty-nine-and-a-half years old.

Example: The most common Roth IRA is established when a person decides to roll over their 401(k). When you decide to roll over your 401(k), you will have to pay taxes on the money before you roll it over if you choose to invest it into a Roth IRA. Once you roll the money over and start the Roth IRA, you will be able to keep the interest and earnings you receive, so when you reach retirement age, you will be able to get all the money without having to pay taxes.

Another tax-advantage product is cash-value life insurance. As I mentioned earlier, you will not have to pay taxes on your money in the cash value part of your policy if you take the money out as a loan or a withdrawal. If you take all of your money out from a cash-value life insurance policy at one time, the insurance company is required to report you to the IRS. As you get older and the money in your cash value builds up, the smart thing to do is to set up a specific amount that you want to receive yearly, also known as an income stream, to avoid paying taxes. Many people use the income stream when they are using the money in their cash value to help pay for their retirement.

Lastly, purchasing a municipal bond is another great way to save on paying taxes. These bonds are issued by a public entity at or below the state level. In most cases, you are exempt from having to pay federal income taxes on the interest you receive from the bonds. Depending on a state's income tax laws, you may be exempt from paying state taxes on your interest as well. It is important that you consider all aspects of a municipal bond before making a purchase because there are instances where the income generated by a municipal bond may be taxable.

When it comes to selecting financial products for your child, you want to make sure you know what tax category it falls in. Unlike taxes that are automatically deducted from your paycheck, parents have control over what products they want to set up for their children to help reach financial goals. Remember it is not only a good thing to help set up financial products for your children, but you should spend time explaining different taxes they will pay once they begin working. Teaching your child about what taxes are and how to use different financial products to stop paying taxes will help them be able to preserve more of their wealth when they get older.

Note: *When you make a policy withdrawal, you are not subject to taxation up to the amount paid into the policy. Anything over the amount you have paid into the policy is subject to taxation.*

8 Money-Making Assets vs. Liabilities

We have all heard the saying "don't put all your eggs in one basket." It is true. When it comes to building wealth, you need to have both long-term and short-term financial products in your portfolio. This will insure you have the appropriate accounts set up for your specific needs. As you are building wealth, it is also important to buy more assets than liabilities.

Liabilities are purchases that don't have potential to generate continuous income. They only subtract money from your cash flow and lose value over time. Most of the items your children purchase when they are young are liabilities. In order to generate as much income as possible, your child should invest in money-making assets. Money-making assets are assets that will help your child produce ongoing income. Before we look at different ways to purchase money-making assets, let's look at an example of how something can be viewed as an asset when it is really a liability.

Most people consider their cars to be an asset because they are necessities that help us go to work and run errands, however they are major liabilities. The value of a car depreciates every day, causing them to be worth less than what you paid for them. You spend a great amount of money on car insurance, maintenance, and repair bills. Most people consider having a car as an unavoidable expense. Even if we may need a car, we can still be smart when it comes to purchasing one.

When you purchase a car, you can either buy it with straight cash or finance it. When you finance the car, you are paying out extra money. As we discussed in chapter five, the negative side of compounding interest causes you to have to pay out more money so the loan company can make an extra profit. I understand sometimes you may not be able to afford buying a car with cash, but if you are privileged to buy your child's first car straight cash you should.

The reason being is the money you can save from not paying extra interest charges. Instead of focusing on paying an expensive car note, your child can use the extra money to invest in money-making assets. If you were going to pay their car note for them, you will be able to save the money and start working on building wealth for yourself.

Money-Making Assets

It is important to help your child understand what money-making assets are so they won't fall into the trap of confusing assets with liabilities. Accumulating assets and limiting your liabilities is the key to building wealth. The difference between poor people and wealthy people is that wealthy people control their money. They let their money work for them and focus on receiving money from assets without being present—what is called residual income. Let's look at some money-making assets that wealthy people invest in.

Real Estate

One of the most popular assets they invest in is real estate. Whether it is a house, condo, apartment, business, or property, they purchase these assets in hope of getting tenants who will consistently pay rent. Since the 2008 recession, there has been some controversy as to whether purchasing real estate is really an asset. I say it all depends on your financial goals and what areas you purchase the real estate in.

The purchase of tax liens has also become popular. Depending on what state you live in, you have the opportunity to bid on unpaid property taxes. Every state is different, but the majority of them will allow you to receive interest on your initial investment or gain ownership of the property if the homeowner does not pay for their taxes by a designated time period. It is a great way to obtain property without having to pay a lot of money.

Gold

When it comes to having recession-proof assets, purchasing gold and silver makes the top of the list. If you were like me, you started to see a lot of We Buy Gold franchises pop up in the last economic downturn. You may have thought it was a great concept because you were receiving cash back, but the owner of the franchise was making a much bigger profit than you could imagine. When economies go down, historically the price of gold goes up. If not, it at least stays the same.

Treasuries

For people who don't have a high risk tolerance who are searching for other assets that can help them accumulate wealth, US default-proof treasury bills, treasury notes, and treasury bonds may appeal to them. As we talked about earlier, when you purchase a bond from the government you receive a set interest rate once the bond matures. Treasury bills are considered short-term investments because they can mature in a matter of days or weeks. Treasury notes, on the other hand, pay every six months and mature after two, three, five, seven, or ten years. Like treasury notes, treasury bonds pay every six months, but they are long-term investments that mature after thirty years.

Foreign Assets

If you are afraid of another recession coming along in the US, you may suggest that your child invest in foreign assets. Since the assets are not affected by what is going on in the US market, your child has an opportunity to still see tremendous growth in their money, even during hard times. When deciding on what countries to invest in, make sure your child researches the history of the country's market.

Don't forget that the Global Index Universal Life products are another tool to use when investing in a foreign market. Because it allows clients to get an interest rate based on how well foreign markets are performing indirectly, your child would still have an opportunity to grow their money in tough economic times. In general, owning any kind of IUL product is a great asset. They give clients all the benefits needed to build wealth, and if something happens to them, they are able to leave money behind for their family to build wealth.

There are other ways to obtain money-making assets that will help your child build wealth, however, these are some common ways to generate income aside from the different financial products we discussed earlier. When your child is ready to go out and make a life for themselves, sharing this information will help them have a clear idea of what direction they should go in to continue building wealth. Help your child understand that real assets help you generate long-term income. Which leads me to my next point: Purchasing money-making assets will help your child have an opportunity to retire younger. Let's look at how that is possible in the next section.

How Assets Have an Effect on Retirement

Have you ever met someone who was always complaining about being broke, but they are the champion of always buying things they want? We all know someone who always complains about being broke, but they always have on a new pair of shoes or the latest outfit. They believe they have time on their side, and the next thing you know, twenty years have passed and they have no retirement in place. In order to plan properly for your financial future, you have to want better for yourself. Many people never get to where they want to be in life because they keep putting things off each day. The spirit of procrastination is the number-one

#yourlifetimecashflow

reason why people fail to obtain their financial goals. Too many people live off of the "now mentality." They look at the way things are today and never plan ahead for their future. Saving money is always an issue for them.

The way to have a successful retirement is to accumulate money-making assets that will allow you to live a comfortable lifestyle when you decide you do not want to work anymore. The majority of people are familiar with the Road of Responsibility and follow it well, but they tend to avoid the Road to Retirement until it is too late to even start. If you have ever wondered why some people don't have to work after they retire from a job and why others do, it is because those who still have to work did not properly plan for their financial future. Most adults past the age of sixty-five would not voluntarily work if they had a choice.

The truth is retirement is a choice. In America, we teach our kids to go to college, get a great paying job, and work there until they reach retirement age. Can I let you in on something? Retirement is not about your age at all. It is about how much money you have that can last you until you pass away. That is why it is important to obtain assets that will help bring you continuous cash flow. If your child wanted to retire when they turned thirty years old, it is possible.

So now you are probably wondering, how is that possible? First, if they don't have the entrepreneurial spirit, they can get into a high-paying career, purchase some money-making assets, and immediately start making their money work for them by purchasing financial products with compounding interest. If they do have an entrepreneurial spirit, they are way ahead of the financial game.

#yourlifetimecashflow

The RRRR Strategy

As we travel in life, there are two roads that we must learn to travel if we want to come out wealthy. Those roads are the Road of Responsibility and the Road to Retirement. It is necessary to help your child understand the importance of traveling down both roads in life, also known as the RRRR strategy. This strategy teaches people how to manage their finances while they are young and to begin saving and accumulating assets at the same time.

The Road of Responsibility helps us see all the financial obligations and liabilities we should work on paying off while we are young. The cycle of most people's lives are when they are young, they don't make a lot of money. They begin to move out of their parent's house and accumulate bills. They have a lot of responsibility, whether it be their house, car, student loans, credit cards, or any other financial obligations.

They get so focused on paying bills and trying to survive that they never turn off the Road of Responsibility and enter the Road to Retirement. The Road to Retirement helps us see that in order to live a comfortable lifestyle when we get older, we also have to start saving our money. While traveling the Road to Retirement, it is smart to begin investing in money-making assets like life insurance, stocks, mutual funds, real estate, IRAs, or any other interest accounts.

As you are paying down your debt and building wealth for yourself, the two roads meet in the middle. When this happens, you have reached what is known as the Intersection of Stability. This is where your responsibilities should be under control and you have to learn how to resist the temptation of refinancing your home or getting into more debt because your financial load is decreasing. This is also the time where financial confidence should be increasing because you should finally be able to see decent returns on your money. Once an individual reaches this intersection, they are well on their way toward financial stability.

Example of RRRR strategy:

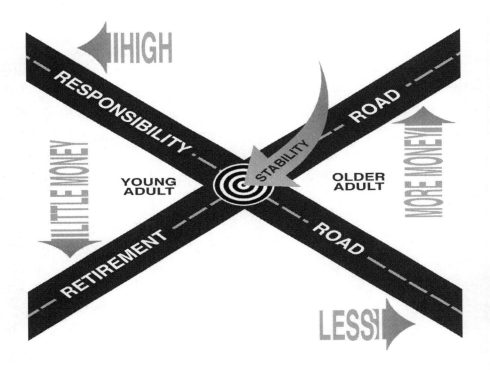

The picture above demonstrates how the RRRR strategy looks. On the left side, you are a young adult. You don't have a lot of money, but you have a lot of responsibility. The right side shows by the time you get older and are ready for retirement, you should have enough money saved to enjoy retirement. At the same time, you should have less responsibility because throughout the years leading to retirement, you should have paid down your debt.

#yourlifetimecashflow

ROAD 1

Road of Responsibility

Financial Obligations:

Rent, Mortgage, Car Note, Credit Cards, Student Loans

When it comes to the Road of Responsibility, you should list all of the major debts you can get rid of after paying the designated payment amount and come up with a plan that works best for you to get the bills paid off as soon as possible. Everyone has different responsibilities, but some common things people put on their list are mortgage payments, car notes, credit cards, and student loans. After you put together a strategy on how to pay those things off, it is important to remember to put together a plan to stay on top of ongoing bills as well. For an example, you may put together a budget where you pay your car insurance or cellphone bill six months in advance to help free up more money to invest toward your retirement.

ROAD 2

Road to Retirement

Financial Products and Property:

Life Insurance, Stocks, Mutual Funds, Annuities, Real Estate

As you enter the Road to Retirement, you should be looking to open financial products that will help you accumulate the most money before you reach your designated retirement age. The faster the product can grow your money, the sooner you can retire. Some common products people invest their money in to help plan for retirement are life insurance with

#yourlifetimecashflow

cash value, stocks, bonds, mutual funds, annuities, and real estate. Remember to rate your risk tolerance before investing in stocks and mutual funds.

Real Life Application

Britany, twenty-three, graduates from college and gets a job making $30,000 a year. She decides she wants to retire by fifty-five. That means she plans on working for thirty-two years. By using the RRRR strategy, Britany will be able to strategize how she plans on meeting her financial goals for retirement. Britany gets a blank sheet of paper and labels it the RRRR strategy. She draws two roads and labels one as the Road of Responsibility and the other as the Road to Retirement. On the Road of Responsibility, Britany focuses on all of the responsibilities she has to pay such as her student loans, mortgage, car note, and other long-term lump-sum expenses.

She begins to put together a plan, based on her paycheck, of the things she wants to get rid of first. She decides to get rid of the smaller debt first so she can use the extra money to pay more towards her bigger debt. She also implements a system to help her pay ongoing expenses in a way that would position her to save more. By focusing on those things first, Britany can create more money to invest in her retirement accounts in later years. After she decides what her strategy will be to pay her long-term expenses and gives herself a date to have those things paid off, she focuses on planning for retirement. She decides since her risk tolerance is not high, she is going to put a small amount of her money in some stock, some in a life insurance product, and some in an annuity.

She chooses three different accounts instead of one because she knows the importance of diversification. She also knows there is a fifty/fifty chance to gain money in a stock. She decides to take a chance, but she opens up the other two financial accounts as a backup in case she loses money in her stock. By sitting down and planning her financial future, Britany has a clear idea what she is working toward and what it will take to retire comfortably with less responsibility.

By applying the RRRR strategy to their lives, your children will be able to experience financial freedom. Paying down your liabilities while building wealth is a crucial step to avoiding the debt trap. Purchasing money-making assets is a sure way to secure your income. The earlier your child understands the steps to building wealth, the more profitable they will be.

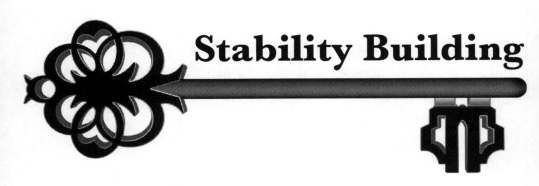

Stability Building

If you want to gain financial stability, you have to have a system in place in order to take control of your financial future the best way possible.- Sheena Robinson

9

Wiping Out Debt

After graduating college, my credit score was 710. My mom helped me raise my score while I was in school, but she forgot to explain how she did it or how to maintain it. After I moved from home, I began making my own financial decisions. I started getting pre-approval letters for credit cards in the mail and started applying for them. Once I got approved, I started maxing out the cards by buying everything I wanted. When it was time to pay the money back, it became hard for me to remain consistent because I didn't budget for the extra credit card bills.

Many of you were like me growing up. You were not educated about how to manage debt or how to establish a high credit score. You saw credit cards as free money and didn't use them appropriately. Now that the roles have reversed, you are in charge of preparing your child to deal with debt. If you are not discussing debt with your child, you are setting them up for financial failure.

#nomoredebt

Good Habits for Debt Avoidance

Some parents don't feel they should discuss their finances with their children, but it is a good idea to have a conversation regardless. It doesn't matter if you use someone else's story to get your point across. The majority of the American people would be better off financially if they were taught debt-prevention techniques. Rather than your child making foolish financial decisions when they are older, it is better to give them the knowledge they need beforehand so they will have a chance to live the best life possible. Let's look at some habits we can start teaching our kids when they are young:

1 Teach them not to overspend.

When you go out shopping with your child, it is a good idea to carry a list in the store. It will help you demonstrate to your child the importance of sticking to your list. After they see you following your list, they will be more likely to repeat the same behavior. As I have already discussed earlier, prepaid debit cards are also another way to help your child from overspending. The more time your child has to practice these habits, the better the chance that they will not overspend when they get older.

2 Teach them about paying people on time.

Teach your children the importance of paying people back. This builds discipline, and it helps instill the trait of responsibility. A great way to help instill the trait is to loan your children money and make them pay it back. By doing so, you will help your children under-

stand that when they ask to borrow money, it means they are ask-
ing with the intention of giving the money back. Helping your child
understand the concept of borrowing will help save them from much
frustration as they get older. The earlier you start to teach this concept, the more time your children will have to practice, which will
help them find it easier to pay people back as adults.

When your children borrow money from you, it is a good idea to give
them a certain date to pay you back if they have any income coming
in. This will help get them used to having a sense of urgency when it
comes to paying people back. Another way to show your child how
to have a sense of urgency is going through your own credit card
statement and showing them your payment due date and allowing
them to watch you make a payment each time it's due. This will help
them see that you actually practice what you preach and make them
more likely to follow in your footsteps.

3 Teach them about not falling into the credit card trap.

As soon as your child turns eighteen, credit card companies bom-
bard them with pre-approved credit card letters. Some companies
go as far as offering free giveaways to college students who open
a card. The issue is not credit cards. The issue we see today is
the lack of knowledge about credit cards. They serve their purpose
whether you use them for an emergency, buying groceries, paying other bills, shopping, or just going on vacations. The spending
abuse has caused several people to think negatively about credit
cards. Many people fall into the trap of overspending, not paying
their bill on time, just paying the minimum, and getting too many
credit cards. Teach your child the proper way to handle their credit

#nomoredebt

card with care.

4 Teach them about never cosigning for anyone!

This is a touchy subject, but I suggest that you teach your child to not allow other people to mess up their credit. I had two experiences where I was talked into cosigning for two boyfriends. That was one of the stupidest things I could have done. I allowed them to make me think they were going to take care of the payments and pay on time. I ended up getting the worst end after breaking up with them because I was still responsible for the items. The only exceptions I would consider are if you are married or you as a parent cosign for your child or vice-versa.

Because many of us don't get the proper knowledge about debt when we are younger, we are left to go out and make poor financial decisions. It is important for parents to begin preparing their children on how to handle real life issues before they leave home. Many adults still suffer today as a result of not being taught debt prevention tactics while they were young.

During the 2008 recession, the unemployment rate began to rise drastically. Families started having to choose between paying their utility bills or making sure they had food to eat. Some people who felt they were financially secure found themselves falling into debt. Some Americans also became homeless. The sudden shift caused a revolution that has challenged us to become more financially informed.

I am a firm believer that the problems families experienced could have been prevented if they had been properly educated about managing their finances. When you think about professionals such as Michael Jordan, who is still a household name today, he did not get this far without practicing his craft. People don't look at managing money as a craft, but it is. How can you expect to be successful and have wealth if you don't know how to acquire it?

What happens when you acquire money and you don't know how to manage it? We have all seen stories where many celebrities have had to file bankruptcy. The first question we ask is how that is possible. They knew how to acquire money, but they were not taught how to properly manage it. Just because someone appears to have money doesn't mean they know how to use it properly.

Debt does not discriminate. It doesn't matter your race, gender, social status, education background, or who your parents are. If you don't know how to manage money, you will find yourself in debt. According to American Household 2014 Statistics, credit card debt ranks the third highest type of debt in households. Only mortgages and student loan debts are higher. The average credit card debt is $15,607.[8]

The problem with using credit cards continues to worsen because the majority of people are not taught beforehand how to use them wisely. It is not until many people get ready to buy a car or make a big purchase that they begin to understand how their credit card habits can affect their credit worthiness. When trying to establish credit, creditors and lenders look at your credit history to determine if you are worthy to extend credit to. Creditors use your credit report to see how you've handled your credit over time.

---

[8] http://www.nerdwallet.com/blog/credit-card-data/average-credit-card-debt-household/

#nomoredebt

A credit report helps creditors determine how much risk they are taking by extending you credit. There are five areas creditors look at. They are the payment history (35 percent), the credit usage (30 percent), the types of accounts you have (10 percent), the length of time you have had the accounts (15 percent), and the new accounts you have applied for (10 percent). It is important that you help your child understand how their credit can affect them.

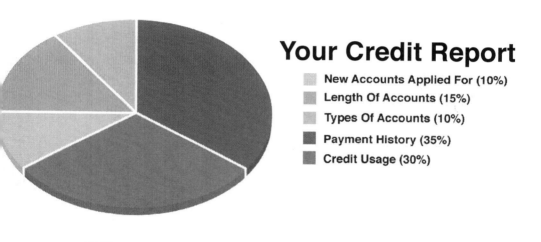

Your Credit Report

- New Accounts Applied For (10%)
- Length Of Accounts (15%)
- Types Of Accounts (10%)
- Payment History (35%)
- Credit Usage (30%)

If your child ever wants to purchase any item, and they don't have the money upfront, then a credit card or installment loan would allow them to use a petty cash system where they make a purchase and pay later. It sounds like an easy thing to do, but many people find themselves in financial jail. In this section we will discuss ways to help your child have a better grip on debt.

Credit Maintenance

In order to help your child build a great credit score, you have to help them understand how they can maintain their credit report. The credit score is determined based on the items in the credit report. Credit scores normally range from 300–850. It is important to go over debt prevention techniques with your child to help them avoid falling into debt. Let's look at some of the things you should go over.

1 When getting a credit card or installment loan, make sure you are getting a low interest rate.

Remember the Rule of 72? In the case of a credit card, the higher your interest rate, the faster your debt can double. When helping your child find a suitable credit card, you should alert your child of cards with high interest rates and yearly fees. These cards trap people into paying more interest because it takes more time to pay them off. A good way to help your child cut down the time they have to pay credit card bills is to teach them how to pay more than just the minimum. You should teach your children to get into the habit of paying at least $30 or more over the minimum payment to cut down on the interest they have to pay back. If your children fall victim to a lot of cards, they should pay the high interest card first to help pay it off faster so they can free up more money to save.

2 Don't open up too many credit card accounts.

It is a good idea to not have more than three credit cards. Even though it is tempting to sign up for a credit card in almost every department store you visit just to receive a discount, it can come back to bite you. The more cards you have increases the chances that you may not be able to pay the money back. If you are not paying your cards on time or you are carrying high balances on your cards, you can affect your credit score tremendously. Make sure your child is not taking on more debt than they can pay back.
#nomoredebt

3 Make payments early.

They should use one card to purchase items or pay bills and pay the bill before the credit card company reports it. By doing so, if your credit card company reports your bill before your due date, it makes it look like you have a balance. But if you pay it before the reporting date, it will not reflect you having a balance. By doing this, the balance on your credit report will always show a $0 balance.

4 Always make a payment.

If your child can't pay the balance off every month, they should at least pay 20–30 percent off of the credit limit. If they get behind paying their bills one month, they should call and see if they can get the late fee waived. Most companies are willing to work with you if that's your first time.

5 Open different types of accounts.

When building credit, lenders like to see that you are well rounded. They like to see you have a variety of accounts such as a credit card, car loan, and an installment loan. More diversity will help you when you are trying to get approved by a lender. They like to see that you can handle both revolving and installment loans.

6 Add utility bills to their credit report.

As long as your child is paying their cable bill, cellphone bill, utility bills, and other bills on time, they should ask the company to report

#nomoredebt

to the credit bureaus to help increase their score.

7 Don't close accounts.

Encourage them not to close their credit card accounts or go over their line of credit. The length of time you are with a company makes up 15 percent of your credit score.

8 Don't consolidate cards if possible.

Teach them not to consolidate their bills onto one card. It is better to have smaller balances on a few cards. The only exception is if they have a higher interest rate on one card and the interest rate on the other card is lower. Of course you want to pay the lowest interest as possible.

9 Monitor your credit ratio on your credit cards.

Your credit ratio is the percentage of your income that is taken up by paying debt. When creditors look at the amount you owe, they are looking at the percentage you have used toward the amount of your credit limit. The goal for your child should be to keep their debt ratio under 30 percent. The higher the ratio, the less chance you have of getting a loan or credit card.

10 Don't apply for too much credit at once.

When you are trying to get approved for a credit card or a loan, you should be careful how many companies you let review your credit.

#nomoredebt

The inquiry the company makes can have a negative effect on your credit score. An inquiry is when the companies refer to a credit bureau to obtain information about your report. The inquiry stays on your credit report for at least two years. Not only does it affect your credit, but it makes you look like you are desperate for credit and no one is accepting you.

11 Monitor identity theft.

Teach them to monitor their credit and check for identity theft and dispute items that they think should not be there. Sometimes you can fix your credit score just by correcting mistakes.

12 Go over different terminology.

When it comes to teaching your child about a credit report, you should help them understand the terminology and how negative items work. By helping them understand terms upfront, they will have a clear idea of the different things they should stay away from. Teaching them what charge-offs, collection agencies, judgements, liens, and repossessions are can help children make better choices when they get older. Let's look at each of these.

Charge-Off
When the original company you have debt with writes your debt off as a loss in their books after it has gone delinquent for a certain amount of time.

Collection Agency
A business that pursues payment for the account you had with the original collector.

Judgement
A court order that gives a creditor the right to collect money from you.   *#nomoredebt*

Lien
> The right someone has to keep your possessions or property until your debt is paid in full.

Repossession
> This is when the dealership you bought your car from takes your car back because of nonpayment.

Bankruptcy
> A legal status you receive when you can't pay back your debt. When you file bankruptcy, you are able to eliminate or repay some of your debt. You are protected from creditors under the protection of the federal bankruptcy court.

Your credit report is important when it comes to renting an apartment, purchasing car insurance, getting a good job, and being able to finance things. If your children are not fortunate enough to pay cash up front for things, not having good credit can make things tough. Teaching your child how to build and maintain their credit is a great start to help them toward financial success. When you teach your child how to understand credit cards and loans early, they avoid becoming a statistic.

10

Entrepreneurship: The New Job Security

The cycle for most people is they graduate high school, attend college or a trade school, and then get a job. Everyone around them encourages them to go work for someone. Very few people grow up with the thoughts of being an entrepreneur. Most of us grow up with an ambition to soar up the corporate ladder.

The truth is that was the standard back in the 1950s, but today the job market has changed drastically. You can no longer put your destiny in your employer's hand. With the rude awakening of the jump in unemployment in the early 2000s, it is no longer safe to say that you will be with the same company your entire career. The lack of job security has caused a number of people to doubt the American pattern of life that they were brought up with.

You can go to college and get a degree and still find yourself in the unemployment line. You can go to college to get a degree and still not get paid what you are worth. Because of massive job layoffs, companies have the upper hand when it comes to the hiring pro-

#youneedaPlanB

cess. With so many companies concerned about their profit, they would rather bring someone on board who will accept a lesser salary than the person who has several degrees.

Because of the competitive job market, it is not uncommon to hear people you know talking about how they want to go back to college and get a degree. Americans have conformed to a way of life that is outdated. You have to move with the times or get left behind. As we discussed in the last chapter, the 2008 recession was a defining moment. It helped many people see that if they want to have job security, they have to do something extra other than working a job.

I was fortunate to attend college and it was a great experience. I learned a lot of great things that have helped me be a well-rounded person. I enjoyed the friendships I built and the overall college experience. I support college, but what I am saying is don't set your children up to believe that they are automatically going to be successful because they have a degree. This only applies to a small percentage of college grads. The majority of them end up in dead-end jobs.

When it comes to taking control of your destiny and making a great amount of money at the same time, entrepreneurship is the way to go. During the recession, I had a friend named Emily who worked as a nurse for over twenty years. She was a faithful employee and always did overtime when she was asked. She gave the company she worked for 100 percent of her efforts, only to be laid off. She was devastated. She found herself struggling to get another job because of all the other job candidates she had to compete against.

Emily felt betrayed that she had been let go when others who didn't work as hard as she did got to stay. After going through a period of unemployment and struggling to find another job, she knew she needed to find a way to make extra income for herself. She decided to start her own online jewelry business. In the beginning, things were slow but they gradually picked up. After being unemployed for two years, she finally received a job offer. She accepted the offer; however, she kept working her business on the side. She was determined to not let another job decide her financial destiny.

There are a lot of other people in the world who experienced losing their job like Emily did. Many of them were not as fortunate. They did not pick themselves up and learn how to start their own thing. They focused only on finding another job. When you only focus on a job and never have a Plan B, it increases the chance that it will be harder to bounce back when you lose a job. Even if you have savings stored up, you will still have to take away money from your cash flow rather than building it. Having a Plan B is the way to go if you want to be an entrepreneur and you are not fully financially stable enough to run your business on a full-time basis. A Plan B is a business you can do aside from your job that helps you supplement your income.

Building an Entrepreneur Spirit Early

When teaching your child how to build wealth for themselves, it is smart to instill an entrepreneurial spirit in them at a young age. Even if your child wants to work for someone when they get older, you should still encourage them to use their talents, sell a product, or do a service on the side to help bring in extra income. It is smart to get your child in the habit of becoming an entrepreneur as early as age five. You can help them come up with a business idea.

The most common ideas are lemonade stands, car washes, bake sales, and making jewelry. Helping your child with one of these ideas can help increase their cash flow. There are several things your child can sell: T-shirts, mugs, picture frames, handbags, key chains, or artwork.

With all the items listed above, your child can personalize or decorate them. Think outside the box and make this a fun experience with your child. As they grow older, you should help them identify a business that they would be successful in, whether it is their main gig or their Plan B.

When you encourage your child to have an entrepreneurial spirit early, they will have a chance to capitalize on more income. Even if they are not able to be an entrepreneur full-time, they should consider doing it part-time. Not only can you make a great amount of money, but you will be able to control your financial destiny. Let's look at some other ways you can benefit from being an entrepreneur.

1 Being an entrepreneur can help you save on paying taxes.

When you have your own small business, you are able to write off your expenses each year. This will give you a greater chance to keep more money instead of paying a penalty because you didn't pay enough in taxes at your job.

2 Being an entrepreneur can also give you an opportunity to capitalize on more income.

There is no cap on your income potential like there is with a job. Even if you have a job, having extra income for yourself gives you "income insurance" in case you were to lose your job. It also helps you grow your wealth faster.

3 If you decide to become an entrepreneur on a full-time basis you will be able to have more autonomy.

Whether you are full-time or part-time, you get to decide when you want to run your business.

4 Entrepreneurship also gives you job security.

No one can hire or fire you.

There are other benefits to being an entrepreneur, but I feel these are the most rewarding. Saving money on taxes, growing extra income, enjoying job security, and having autonomy are all things many people who work regular jobs are looking for. When you want to become wealthy, you need to find ways to help you bring in extra cash flow. Having more money also gives your child the opportunity to retire sooner.

Entrepreneurship comes with a lot of perks, but your child needs to be willing to be disciplined and work hard to reach their financial goals. Very few things in life are handed to you. You have to be willing to put in the work to get your desirable result. If your child is willing to put in the work, being an entrepreneur on a full-time basis can be very worthwhile.

Helping your child build habits of an entrepreneur when they are young will make it easier for them to carry those same habits as an adult. Life is unpredictable, and you can't assume you will be in the same career forever and be able to make the amount of money you actually desire. You have to be willing to go after what you want. Even if your child decides to work for someone when they get older, instilling an entrepreneurial spirit in your child early can help allevi- ate a lot of stress for them in the future.

11

The Financial Power System

Have you ever noticed when you walk into a Walmart Super Center anywhere in the United States that they are all similar? When you walk in, you are normally welcomed to the store by the greeter. The store is broken up into different departments that help customers identify their needs more effectively. Once you are ready to check out, you are able to check yourself out or go to a cashier.

Most people don't realize that Walmart Super Centers were strategically designed to all look the same way. By having a similar setup and operating the same way, the owner of the chain is able to create more stores at a faster speed. Because of the powerful Walmart system, the owner can stay consistent with how every store is ran and make sure everyone is following the same procedures.

The same is true for McDonald's franchises. McDonald's is able to make a lot of money because of their powerful system as well. No matter where you go in the world, if you stop at a McDonald's, the food tastes the same. You don't have to be a genius to be a successful worker there—all you have to do is follow the system. If you want to be small, you don't have to have a system. If you want to have an opportunity to succeed in life, you will put a system in place that will help you run things more smoothly. The beauty of a system is you can have one franchise in California and one in Atlanta and still be able to run them the same way by incorporating a system.

Many people wonder why they are not where they thought they would be in life financially. The reason is that they don't have a system in place to help them manage their money. A system is a way to save you time, energy, and money. If you think about the most successful businesses, they all have to have a system they follow.

As we talked about earlier, setting the standards about saving at an early age to your child will create an innate feeling about making better financial decisions. Everyone is a product of a system, whether it is the government system or the school systems. People don't think about being a product of a system because they have been taught that certain systems are requirements for the American people. These systems have to be followed rather you agree or disagree.

If you want to be financially successful, you have to follow a financial system. The system that I recommend is the 70/10/10/10 system, also known as the Financial Power System. This system will allow your child to manage their finances in an orderly fashion as an adult. The system shows your child how to separate their money by putting it into four different categories. Seventy percent of their profit goes to their bills and living expenses. Ten percent goes into an account, such as a savings account, where they are earning interest on the funds. Ten percent goes toward a charity or tithes and the

#systemsgrowmoney

other ten percent is split between building an emergency fund and doing whatever they want to do with the extra money *(this could also be set up as a fun account).*

Example:
The Financial Power System: Salary $1,050

PAY YOURSELF FIRST *(Interest Account)* 10 percent $105	TITHES/ SPECIAL CAUSE 10 percent $105
EMERGENCY FUND / EXTRA ACCOUNT 10 percent $105	RENT, CREDIT CARDS, CAR INSURANCE, CAR NOTE, ETC. 70 percent $735

This example shows you how a person with a $1,050 bi-weekly income breaks each paycheck up. In this scenario $105 *(ten percent)* went toward their interest account to help them utilize the concept of pay yourself first. The next $105 *(ten percent)* went toward a special cause they believed in. Another $105 *(ten percent)* was used to fund both their emergency account and their extra account where they can use the money for whatever they want, and the re-maining $735 *(seventy percent)* went toward their living expenses.

This system gives you power because it helps you prioritize how you will budget your money and it helps you stay organized. When you "walk the walk" and follow the system, you will have financial success because you will have better control of your money. You also want to continue educating yourself on the best products to use to reach your financial goals. Once you have a system to follow, you should continue to repeat it for the best results.

As your child masters the system, they will become more financially stable. The savings in the interest account could be used as an additional emergency fund, a retirement account, or a down payment for a house or a car. Having this type of account will help your child continue to remain disciplined when it comes to the concept of "pay yourself first."

Although your child should save as much as possible toward their future, they should not forget to give back to others. It is true that it is better to give than receive, but it is also true that what goes around comes around. Giving to special causes or tithing gives you a feeling of warmth in knowing you are making a difference in the life of others. It is important that your child grows up with an attitude of gratitude. What good is it to have all the money in the world and have no one to share it with? In the midst of setting your child up for financial success, you should instill humanitarian habits.

While you are helping your children understand the importance of giving back, it is also important to teach them how to put money away in an emergency account. This will help them stay prepared for any unexpected circumstances. Even though it is important for your child to save money as an adult, it is also important that you teach them how to enjoy life. Who said you could not enjoy doing things in life you have always wanted to do? Teach your children to set aside a special fund where they save for the things they want to do in life. Help your child to understand that saving is not to make

#systemsgrowmoney

their life miserable, but to give them a platform to accomplish their future financial goals so they can avoid making the same mistakes many people in the world have already made.

What System to Use

When your child is between the ages of two to eighteen, they should be focused on the 60/20/10/10 system. Because most children in this age group are not paying bills, this system allows them to practice saving and spending. This system suggests that 60 percent of the money your child gets goes into an scheduled account, 20 percent goes toward their fun account, 10 percent goes toward their emergency account, and 10 percent goes toward a special cause/tithes. If your child does pay bills, they should use the 70/10/10/10 system.

Starting a system with your child at a young age will not only help them accumulate money while they are young, but by the time they are an adult they can begin to see the benefits of paying themselves first and continue to practice the habit. If you teach your child to save $30 dollars a month *(roughly a dollar a day)*, that equals $360 a year. Say you made them do this for ten years *(from eight to eighteen years old)* that would equal $3600. They would be able to take that money and invest it in an account giving them compounding interest and start out their adulthood with a down payment to be successful.

Another way to set your child up for success is to take that $30 a month and let them contribute to the scheduled account you opened with compound interest when they were born. Using either method would help set your child up for a better financial outcome than most young people will have when they are ready to leave home. The number one thing successful people have in common is that they have people and their money working for them. You can cut down on the amount of time you work just by having a system in place to help you reach your financial goals.

CHAPTER 12

Benefits of Financial Parenting

When a child graduates high school, it is one of the most defining moments for many parents. They feel as if a burden has been lifted, and they are free to start living their own lives again. The sacrifice parents go through to raise a successful child is often overlooked. Graduation day is often seen as a time of reflection on how well the child has done with the help of their parents.

Parents have to ask themselves if they taught their children the best in order to go out and make a decent life for themselves. Most of them feel like they did, but in reality they failed to teach them how to manage money. It doesn't seem like a big deal when the child is growing up because parents don't immediately see the result of what happens without teaching financial education. It is not until their child starts experiencing life that they realize their child is lacking financial skills.

That is why it is so important for you to incorporate financial parenting at a young age. Molding your child throughout their childhood ensures they will be well prepared to live the best life possible after they walk across that graduation stage.

#raiseuparichkid

The Nine Benefits of Financial Parenting

Financial parenting gives your child a chance to learn financial education, and it also benefits you as a parent in the long run. Let's look at some of the two-way benefits of financial parenting.

1 Financial parenting helps create a financially secure child.

When you teach your child about money when they are young, they learn the value of saving. They have a longer time to generate income for themselves and to use their money more effectively. Teaching them about different financial products helps them understand the importance of gaining interest to help generate the most income as possible. They also learn the importance of diversifying their money and not putting it all in one place.

#raiseuparichkid

When children are able to manage their money correctly, they will be more likely to be able to care for their aging parents. Have you ever wondered why so many adults neglect taking care of their parents? Many of them neglect to taking care of their parents because they are not financially able to. When they don't have to worry about how they will pay their own bills, they can focus more on making sure their parents are well taken care of.

2 Financial parenting helps with decision making.

As we discussed earlier, most children are victims to impulse buying. Because they have never been challenged to think through their spending decisions, they fall into the trap of thinking they can get whatever they want, whenever they want. Financial parenting teaches your child how to avoid instant gratification and to think about the consequences before they purchase an item. Giving your child a chance to learn through trial and error is the best way for them to make better money decisions.

In life, mistakes are the best-taught lessons. As parents, you have to be consistent with teaching your child why certain decisions are not the best ones. It is so much more effective to begin teaching your child how to make better spending decisions at an early age, so they will make better choices as an adult. It pays off when you can trust your child to make better decisions when you are not around.

3 Financial parenting helps build a strong work ethic.

When you require your child to help contribute toward purchases made for them, it helps create a strong work ethic. You help set the expectation that you have to work for what you want in life. When I was told I would have to pay my own car note and car insurance when I got my first car, I took ownership of my car because it was actually my money being spent. I didn't mind going to work because I knew I had an obligation to take care of.

Trust me, it can make a big difference in the attitude of your child when things are handed to them and when they are required to work for what they want. Because of my experience, I have a greater appreciation for life and the things I am able to buy on my own. It is important that parents teach their child that there is a tradeoff between getting what you want in life and working for it. It makes your job easier as a parent because your child will not always expect you to do everything for them.

4 Financial parenting builds discipline.

If you recall your childhood, there were some things your parents required of you that you still incorporate in your life today. Even though we hate to admit, it was the things our parents constantly annoyed us about that became habits. Imagine if they did the same thing as a financial parent. You might not have liked them nagging you about saving, but by the time you were an adult, you would have bought into the concept.

The reason being is that you would have had a chance as an adult to reap the benefits of what you did when you were younger. Most of us are visual people. It is not until we see things come to pass that we jump on board to consistently do them. Because it is harder to see immediate results from saving as an adult, it is harder to become disciplined to start saving. When you teach your child financial discipline, they are less reluctant to become disciplined in other areas in their life.

5 Financial parenting passes down wealthy habits for generations to come.

Most of us were not fortunate enough to grow up with a financial education, but who's to say you can't help change the direction of your family. Teaching financial education not only helps elevate your child to a higher level, but it gives your child a chance to continue the legacy. If we don't decide to stand up for what we believe and take action, we will continue to allow our families to struggle.

It amazes me that people think life is about working for someone all their life and struggling to pay bills. I hear people always complaining they want better for themselves, but they are not willing to make a change. Whether it is fear or lack of commitment, no great change comes without having a will-do attitude. Are you determined to make your mark and leave a legacy for your family when you are no longer here on earth? Will you be the game changer by passing down the information needed to help lead more members of your family to financial success?

6 Financial parenting helps you have a closer relationship with your child.

Financial parenthood requires you to spend a great amount of time educating your children. When you set aside time to invest in helping your child have the best life possible, they feel valued. The time you spend with your child will give them an opportunity to open up to you about any concerns they may have. Sharing your money story and mistakes you made when you were young will help them have a greater connection to you.

Your relationship with your child is like any other relationship you have. There has to be communication to establish a bond. The more information you share with your child, the more influence you will have on them. You will be the person they consult when they have financial questions.

7 Financial parenting helps your child live a better quality of life.

Most parents want their kids to live a better life than they did. Financial parenting gives you an opportunity to do just that. When they are financially educated, they can make better decisions for themselves. They will be able to avoid living in debt and actually enjoy life.

The quality of life for many Americans has diminished because they feel trapped by their financial situation. If they didn't have a job, they would risk losing everything. A lot of people are just one paycheck from being homeless. Because of that, there are many people working jobs they hate and repeating the cycle year after year. Financial parenting allows your child to have a chance to live a comfortable lifestyle.

8 Financial parenting teaches your child how to reach their financial goals in life.

#raiseuparichkid

Many people have dreams, but not too many people put together a plan to reach those dreams. A dream without a plan of action is very unlikely to happen. Financial parenting helps you teach your child how to set goals and map out how they will reach them. It also teaches them how to set specific goals that they can attain in a reasonable amount of time.

When your children learn how to make the right financial decisions, they are less likely to ask you and debt collectors for money. When you require your child to be accountable, they are held to a higher standard and are more likely to reach their goals. Reaching more goals in life will make your child happy. As a result, they will keep you happy.

9   Financial parenting helps your child avoid a lifestyle of debt.

Living a lifestyle of debt is like living in fear. People living in debt are constantly trying to avoid bill collectors. They screen all of their calls before they answer the phone. Do you know someone like this? Some people become so stressed to the point that their health is affected.

One of the biggest benefits of financial parenting is that it teaches debt prevention. Programs like the Financial Head Start Program were designed to help steer your child into the right financial direction. Upon completing the program, your child will be able to make more-educated financial decisions. When your child makes the right financial decisions, they will ask you for less money, and debt collectors won't be calling your house looking for them.

#raiseuparichkid

As you can see, there are several benefits to becoming a financial parent. If you feel as if you are not in the best financial position before you start, I challenge you to learn for yourself as you teach. Don't allow your child to become financially unstable because you don't have time, you don't believe you are qualified to teach them, or you feel like money shouldn't be discussed with your children. I challenge you to think of all the benefits you and your children will receive by investing in financial education.

It is up to the parents whether or not their children financially succeed. What parent will you be? Will you be the parent to change the financial well-being of your child? Will you be the parent who still thinks financial parenting is not necessary for your child's overall financial success? The things we discussed in this book were to help you get started to becoming a financial parent.

Now that you have all the tools you need to get started, welcome to financial parenthood.

Bibliography

1. http://www.councilforeconed.org/policy-and-advocacy/survey-of-the-states/

2. http://www.ryot.org/gallup-poll-70-americans-disengaged-jobs/376177

3. http://www.financialeducatorscouncil.org/financial-literacy-statistics/

4. http://phx.corporate-ir.net/phoenix.zhtml?c=70667&p=irol-newsArticle&ID=1596344&highlight

5. http://money.cnn.com/2012/06/25/pf/emergency-savings/

6. http://www.savingforcollege.com/intro_to_529s/does-a-529-plan-affect-financial-aid.php

7. http://www.treasurydirect.gov/indiv/research/indepth/ebonds/res_e_bonds.htm

8. http://www.nerdwallet.com/blog/credit-card-data/average-credit-card-debt-household/

Notes From The Author

As the author of Financial Parenthood, it is my hope that you walk away empowered to make a change in your household. Engaging in financial parenting is a Personal Decision. As you take the necessary steps to incorporate this type of parenting into your everyday life, it is important to remain consistent with your children. If you are a parent who is always on the go, you may decide to start by selecting one day during the week where you really focus on incorporating financial education. Everyone will have a different way of doing things based on their children, but the important thing is that you stay committed to becoming a financial parent.

When it comes to building your child's mindset, you have to be strategic with what you are depositing into their mental bank account. When you place the right financial information on the inside, it will show in their financial decisions on the outside. The way they perceive their financial life will impact generations to come. You play the biggest role in your child's financial journey because they are watching you to see what they should be doing. Remember: Be intentional!

As parents, I encourage you to start working on your children's physical bank account while they are still in the womb. What types of financial accounts would you like them to have? You should be proactive in putting together a financial plan that you will be able to execute full force once they are born. While planning your children's accounts, it is just as important to make sure you have your own legacy accounts in place to make sure that your children will be taken care of in case you are no longer here.

When you plan ahead for your children's future, they are positioned to have the best life possible. I am not saying children shouldn't have to work for what they want, but I am saying parents should play a more instrumental part in helping their children become financially successful. It is my hope that you take the information given in this book and really take the necessary action and embrace financial parenting. I wish you the best!

Sincerely,

Sheena Robinson

About the Author

Being in the financial industry since 2008, Sheena has been able to help others through financial education. She is very committed to giving back to young people through her 4-part Financial Head-start Series. She is committed to serving churches, nonprofits, and schools to make sure their youth have the ability to soar to greater heights in their finances.

Since launching the program, she has found that many students don't have any idea about basic financial concepts. Within the program, she focuses on keeping things clear, simple, and to the point, so that students find it doable. She is very passionate about seeing a change in the 21st Century youth and their financial habits. Her goal is to make sure by the time they complete the program they are more prepared to make better financial decisions.

She is also the founder of Diva 4 Wealth, an organization dedicated to helping women become financially savvy. She is dedicated to being the change she wants to see revolving around financial education. She is also the host of "Heart2Heart with Shee", an internet talk show that focuses on the issues that teens and young adults face daily. She has a heart for others and enjoys living out her passion by making a difference in their lives.

To learn more about Sheena, please visit financialparenthood.com. If you'd like to contact Sheena directly, she can be reached at 404-980-3511 or sheena@financialparenthood.com. You can connect with her online at www.connecttoshee.com.

35738577R00097

Made in the USA
San Bernardino, CA
02 July 2016